40
INSTANT STUDIES

TRUE TO LIFE
STORIES THAT
CHALLENGE
TEENS TO ENGAGE
CULTURE

BIBLETRUTHS

Standard®
PUBLISHING
Bringing The Word to Life
Cincinnati, Ohio

Published by Standard Publishing, Cincinnati, Ohio
www.standardpub.com

Printed in: USA
Project editor: Jim Eichenberger
Cover and interior design: Symbology Creative

ISBN 978-0-7847-2300-5

15 14 13 12 11 10 09   9 8 7 6 5 4 3 2 1

CONTENTS

■ **How to Use This Book** **6**

■ **Can the devil make me do it?** **7**
Acts 13:4-12; 2 Corinthians 4:4; 11:3
We must recognize and resist the work of our enemy.

■ **How should I respond to temptation?** **9**
Luke 4:1-13
We can be prepared to withstand a test of our faith.

■ **Are there really angels?** **11**
Psalm 148:2-5; Daniel 4:13; Hebrews 1:14
Angels are real and have important jobs to do.

■ **Should I be afraid of demons?** **13**
James 2:19; 1 Timothy 4:1-5; Acts 19:13-16
Demons are real, but they are no match for Jesus.

■ **Am I helpless against evil?** **15**
Ephesians 6:10-18
We are in a war that our leader has already won!

■ **How can I make it through the day?** **17**
1 Corinthians 2:1-10
God loves you! Why not love yourself?

■ **Why didn't God make me beautiful?** **19**
1 Peter 3:1-8
God considers inner beauty more important than physical beauty.

■ **Am I arrogant, or do I just have healthy self-esteem?** **21**
1 Peter 5:5, 6; Proverbs 16:18, 19
God wants us to be humble, not proud.

■ **What is my responsibility to others?** **23**
Philippians 2:4; Psalm 112:5; Acts 20:35
We are not number one!

■ **Why shouldn't I just follow the crowd?** **25**
Exodus 32:1-9, 35; Proverbs 29:25; Romans 12:2
Following the crowd may be easy, but it is dangerous.

■ **Does anyone care that I'm alive?** **27**
Psalm 73:21-26
A friendship with God will conquer loneliness.

■ **What makes a real friend?** 29
Philemon 8-16; Hebrews 10:24
Christian friends are invaluable!

■ **What about cliques?** 31
Acts 9:26-28; Romans 15:5-7
God can bless us through new and unexpected friendships.

■ **How can I recognize true love?** 33
1 John 4:7-21
God defines "true love" differently than this world does.

■ **Do I love people or use them?** 35
Romans 13:8; 1 Corinthians 10:24; 1 Peter 3:7
Mutual respect forms a foundation for strong relationships.

■ **Is sexual purity really such a big deal?** 37
1 Thessalonians 4:1-8
Moral purity is vital in a corrupt world.

■ **Does homosexuality fit into God's plan?** 39
1 Corinthians 6:9-11
Homosexuality violates God's design for humanity.

■ **Is abortion always a bad choice?** 41
Psalm 12:5; Psalm 139:13-16; Jeremiah 1:4, 5
Abortion kills what God values.

■ **How can I improve my relationships with others?** 43
Titus 2:11, 12; 1 Peter 3:3, 4; Job 31:1; James 3:17
Healthy relationships just don't "happen;" they are developed.

■ **What about hypocrites?** 45
Matthew 23
Hypocrisy isn't on God's agenda. Let's be hypocrisy free.

■ **Does the Bible talk about racial prejudice?** 47
Numbers 12:1-15; Revelation 7:9
All human beings have value to God.

■ **Does my reputation matter?** 49
Titus 2:6-8
Many things can attack our integrity—we must guard our godly reputations.

■ **How does God want me to care for my body?** 51
Exodus 23:12; Proverbs 18:9; Ecclesiastes 10:16, 17
Taking care of our bodies honors the one who made them.

■ **Can I be free from bad habits?** 53
Proverbs 20:1; 31:4, 5; Romans 13:12-14; Ephesians 5:4; James 1:26
Destructive habits keep us from being all God wants us to be.

■ **Are my feelings valid?** 55
Psalm 73:2, 3, 13-17, 25, 26
Unchecked emotions will deceive us.

■ **Why did God make me such a failure?** 57
1 Samuel 30:1-19
We can learn to overcome setbacks.

■ **Why aren't there ever enough hours in my day?** 59
Ecclesiastes 11:9; 12:1; John 9:4
Let's seek God's wisdom in managing our moments.

■ **Why should I study?** 61
Proverbs 1:1-7
Serious study brings blessings from God.

■ **How can I make a difference in the world?** 63
Leviticus 19:32-34; Matthew 5:13-16; 1 Thessalonians 4:11, 12; 1 Peter 2:17
Godly attitudes and actions cause communities to take notice.

■ **Does God have a special purpose for me?** 65
Joshua 1:1-7
Join in the work that God is doing in this world.

■ **Has my dysfunctional family warped me for life?** 67
2 Kings 11:1-4, 19-21; 12:1, 2
Hardships arise in even the best of families.

■ **Why should I respect authority?** 69
Romans 13:3-7
When we respect authority, everyone benefits.

■ **How can I keep my temper?** 71
James 1:19-21
We *can* manage our anger.

■ **Is it OK to be angry sometimes?** 73
Ephesians 4:25-28
Anger is not a sin!

■ **How can I heal a broken relationship?** 75
Matthew 18:15-20
The church has always been in the conflict resolution business.

■ **How can we say that Jesus is the only way to Heaven?** 77
Acts 4:12; Luke 12:8-9; John 10:7-11
There is one way to Heaven. His name is Jesus.

■ **How does Islam differ from Christianity?** 79
Matthew 12:1, 2, 7, 8; John 4:21; 1 Peter 2:21-23
Biblical Christianity and Islam disagree about how a person gets right with God.

■ **How does Wicca differ from Christianity?** 81
Psalm 8:4-8; Acts 17:24, 25; Romans 8:20-22
Biblical Christianity and Wicca conflict in their understanding of the natural world.

■ **Should I use the Internet?** 83
Proverbs 1:10, 11, 18, 19; Matthew 10:26, 27; Ephesians 5:15, 16
Let us explore cyberspace wisely.

■ **Does God approve of my music?** 85
Psalm 1:1-3; 137:7-9; Song of Songs 4:1-3
Music is a gift of God that can reach into our emotional depths.

■ **Indexes** 87

HOW TO USE THIS BOOK

IT'S AN AGE OF ENDLESS INFORMATION, AND STUDENTS ARE OVERWHELMED. FURTHERMORE, THEY HAVE A HARD TIME UNDERSTANDING HOW—AND EVEN *IF*—ALL THAT THEY KNOW FITS TOGETHER. THEY ARE DROWNING IN THE FLOOD OF DATA THAT POURS FORTH FROM THEIR MEDIA-RICH YET WISDOM-POOR WORLD.

Help them make a significant connection between the Bible and culture with **40 Instant Studies: Bible Truths**. Each two-page study is easy to prepare, yet rich with true-to-life relevance and biblical depth.

This book is designed as a resource for those in student ministry. In this volume you will find 40 easy-to-prepare lessons that can be used in a pinch or as a part of a larger strategy you have in mind. Each lesson contains:

A REAL STORY

Each lesson is contained on the front and back sides of a single sheet. Remove a lesson by tearing on the handy perforations and head to the copy machine. Make a copy of the introductory story and discussion questions for each student. Start your lesson with high student interest and involvement.

AN EASY-TO-FOLLOW LESSON PLAN

Keep the back page of the lesson to help you guide your group through a Bible study that addresses the questions raised by the introductory article. At your fingertips you have probing discussion questions and clear Scripture commentary.

A CLOSING CHALLENGE

A good Bible study should inspire one to action. At the end of each lesson is a simple activity designed to give your students something concrete to do as a result of the study. These challenges use a variety of teaching methods, but are always focused and memorable.

In addition, find a quick summary of each lesson in the table of contents. Search the Scripture index for specific Bible references used, the story index for the topics covered in the introductory activity, or the topic index to find how specific scriptural themes are handled. You will find a wealth of teaching resources at your fingertips.

In an age of information glut, you need a way to grab the attention of your students and help them apply God's Word to the world around them. Do exactly that with **40 Instant Studies: Bible Truths**.

THE BIG TRUTH

WE MUST RECOGNIZE AND RESIST THE WORK OF OUR ENEMY.

CONFIDENTIAL SOURCE:
ACTS 13:4-12;
2 CORINTHIANS
4:4; 11:3

Can the devil make me do it?

Spacey Strategies

Several years ago, Mojave Aerospace Ventures launched SpaceShipOne and grabbed the $10 million coveted Ansari X Prize. With designer Burt Rutan leading the way, the group completed the requirements and successfully sent up two manned rocket trips into space within one week's time. Here is some background information on this monumental event:

Strategy for the contest: Peter Diamandis came up with the contest idea to help kick-start space tourism. He wanted to encourage more non-government organizations to try their hand at space travel. Peter got the contest idea from the $25,000 Orteig Prize for airplane travel, which was offered in 1919 and won in 1927 by Charles Lindbergh. That contest hastened the beginning of commercial plane travel. Peter would love to see the same thing happen with space travel.

Strategy for fuel: There were twenty-six teams around the globe that had been vying for the prize. Each had its own formula for the necessary fuel to propel its rocket into space. The Mojave team combined two harmless substances—nitrous oxide (also known as laughing gas) and rubber. When the two elements are together, they explode. The fuel tank of SpaceShipOne was filled with nitrous oxide and a hollow tube from the tank to the engine was filled with solid rubber. Although the exact amount is kept secret, the explosive force says it all!

Strategy for takeoff: The competing teams had their own ideas for takeoff as well. Many tried the NASA method of vertical liftoff and varied the format somewhat. One tried to strap the rocket to a balloon that would take it to a certain height and then let the rocket blast off from there. But the winning Mojave team strapped its rocket to the belly of an airplane. The White Knight flew SpaceShipOne to about 50,000 feet. There the rocket ignited and flew off faster than a bullet shoots out of a rifle.

Pilot Michael Melvill flew SpaceShipOne in a few test runs early on and then completed the first of the two contest flights. There were atmospheric elements that caused the rocket to unexpectedly do twenty-nine barrel rolls as it shot from the White Knight. But Michael was OK and the trip went past the required height of 62.5 miles, which is the official worldwide accepted height of where "space" truly begins. Brian Binnie was chosen as the pilot for the flight. He flew SpaceShipOne seventy miles, going eight miles beyond the contest's requirement, and completed the second flight within a week's time.

QUESTIONS TO CONSIDER:

■ What do you think of Peter Diamandis's motivation for creating the contest? Do you think space travel being available to everyone is good or bad? Explain your answers. The article mentioned three different strategies. Share your thoughts on the strategies of the contest, the fuel source, and the takeoff technique. Which surprised you? What would you have tried?

■ Why is a strategy necessary for any venture?

■ Humans aren't the only ones with strategies. God tells us in the Bible that Satan has a strategy to deceive. Let's take a look at that strategy and expose the devil's schemes.

BIBLE TRUTHS

BIBLE**TRUTH** 1

Satan tries to keep the unbeliever from knowing God. ACTS 13:4-7; 2 CORINTHIANS 4:4

■ **What are some distractions in our world today that keep unbelievers from hearing God's words?**

INSIDE STORY: The first priority of Satan is to keep people from seeing the light of Christ at all. Paul wrote that Satan blinded the minds of unbelievers and left them in darkness (2 Corinthians 4:4). This isolates people making it hard to escape darkness, because others in the same situation surround them. They become like one blind man trying to lead another (Matthew 15:14). Furthermore, those who walk "around in the darkness" are not only hostile to God, but become hateful to each other, furthering Satan's plans of destruction (1 John 2:11).

Satan likes to blind powerful people to the truth. Paul went to Paphos, the headquarters of Roman rule in Cyprus. The Roman ruler there, Sergius Paulus, was an intelligent man who wanted to know the truth. But Satan took special care to keep Paulus blind by assigning a special agent of his to this ruler (Acts 13:7).

BIBLE**TRUTH** 2

Satan tries to prevent Christians from reaching honest seekers. ACTS 13:8-12

■ **Do you feel free to share your faith wherever you go? If not, what holds you back?**

INSIDE STORY: But those in darkness long to find the light of the world. When that happens, Satan tries to keep Christians from honest seekers. In Acts 13:8-12, the name of the devil's agent in Paulus' court was Bar-Jesus (meaning "son of Jesus"). This man also called himself Elymas, which means "wise man" or "sorcerer." Elymas "tried to turn the proconsul from the faith" (v. 8), by using deceit and deception (v. 10). This renegade Jew, a false prophet who had abandoned God, was used by Satan to try to block access to an honest seeker.

Throughout the book of Acts we see Satan using people in authority to silence the message of Christ. The Sadducees arrested the disciples and threw them in jail (5:17, 18). Saul, before he was a Christian himself, made "murderous threats" against Christians and arrested them (9:1, 2). Herod had James, the brother of John, beheaded as a show of raw power against the church (12:1, 2).

BIBLE**TRUTH** 3

Satan tries to confuse the minds of Christians.
2 CORINTHIANS 11:3

■ **Imagine that a non-Christian friend tells you that Christianity cannot be true because Christians do not agree with one another. How valid is that argument in your opinion?**

INSIDE STORY: If Satan cannot keep unbelievers blind or keep Christians from sharing the gospel, he tries to lead Christians astray. Ever since Eve, the devil has been trying to convince God's people that they do not need to listen to him (11:3). Satan used the sensuality prevalent in Greece to confuse the Corinthians and legalism in Galatia to trick Christians there (Galatians 1:6, 7; Acts 15:5). He used false teachers and their myths to deceive Christians who lived among those who followed Greek mystery religions in Asia Minor (2 Peter 2:1-3).

Although there is only one gospel, Satan tries to break the unity and disrupt the peace of the church (Ephesians 4:3-6). He knows that the unity of Christians in their common faith glorifies God and convinces the world that God sent Jesus (John 17:2, 23). He fears believers who are united in their thinking (1 Corinthians 1:10; 2 Corinthians 13:11; Philippians 2:2). Satan loves to divide Christians over inconsequential matters and with false doctrine to splinter the church of Christ.

CHALLENGE Ask students what a football coach would do if he had a copy of his opponent's playbook. Review the playbook of Satan discussed in this lesson, and huddle together to call plays to counter it.

How should I respond to temptation?

WE CAN BE PREPARED TO WITHSTAND A TEST OF OUR FAITH.

The Hunt Is Off

Several years ago when the American political scene was focused upon a hotly contested Presidential election and war in Iraq, quite a different political controversy was approaching a showdown in Great Britain. What was this important issue? The British government battled over whether or not to ban the traditional sport of foxhunting.

Next to tea and crumpets, there is surely no more distinctive image of England than the foxhunt. Yet this practice experienced its moment of truth in the United Kingdom.

Earlier a plan to allow only licensed foxhunts was rejected by the elected lawmakers, the House of Commons. A few months later, they voted to ban foxhunting altogether. Thousands of pro-hunting protestors filled Parliament Square that day. During that session, protesters stormed the Commons chamber. The session had to be suspended for over a half hour while protesters were arrested and physically removed from the scene.

At the end of that night, it was agreed that foxhunting would be banned, but the law would not take effect until July 2006. By keeping the bill from being implemented until after the next election, it was hoped that it would prevent further protests and civil disobedience.

Nevertheless the unelected lawmaking body, the House of Lords, considered a legal maneuver that forced the House of Commons either to accept licensed hunting or enforce the ban immediately.

Foxhunter Michael Collins pledged to defy the foxhunting ban if it were enforced. "It's an immoral law," he said, "and I don't recognize immoral laws of any sort." Mike Hobday, of the League Against Cruel Sports, said that pro-hunting protesters "have no respect for the police, no respect for law and order and no respect for parliamentary democracy."

The Hunting Act 2004 went into effect on February 18, 2005. Although more than thirty people have been arrested for violating the law, police generally consider its enforcement to be a low priority.

QUESTIONS
TO CONSIDER:

■ What is meant by the phrase "moment of truth"? Why might this controversy be called a "moment of truth for foxhunting"? How has the practice changed because of the law? How did lawmakers try to postpone this moment of truth?

■ Looking back on your life, think of a crucial decision that you had to make. How is your life different now because of your decision? Was it a decision you could have avoided or postponed? Explain.

■ This controversy caused changes in England. But there have been much greater showdowns in history. The Bible tells us one of the most important moments of truth that ever occurred. It took place when Satan tempted Jesus. Jesus did not try to postpone it, but met it boldly.

BIBLE TRUTHS

BIBLE**TRUTH** 1

Satan attempts to use our natural drives against us. LUKE 4:1-4

■ **How do our natural drives tempt us to reject God? What does that say about our faith?**

INSIDE STORY: Satan often approaches at moments when our natural hungers seem to have control over us. Jesus was hungry from his fast. Satan challenged him to turn a stone into bread, suggesting he might die without food. Jesus refuted that idea by quoting Scripture (Deuteronomy 8:3). This idea is echoed elsewhere in Scripture. David was a lonely and probably hungry fugitive when Saul was in power. During these weak moments David wrote, "Taste and see that the LORD is good" (Psalm 34:8). Later David would repeat this theme. "How sweet are your words to my taste . . . therefore I hate every wrong path" (Psalm 119:103, 104). When tempted to let physical needs drive him, David testified that only God's Word truly satisfied. Solomon remembered his father's words when he advised young men in his day. "Honey from the comb is sweet to your taste. Know also that wisdom is sweet to your soul . . . and your hope will not be cut off" (Proverbs 24:13, 14).

BIBLE**TRUTH** 2

Satan tries to get us to sacrifice our values for power. LUKE 4:5-8

■ **What types of power do you long for? What are legitimate and illegitimate ways of attaining power?**

INSIDE STORY: Satan promised power to Jesus in exchange for his submission to him, offering a crown without a cross. Jesus again responded by quoting Scripture (Deuteronomy 6:13). Bowing down to Satan would be sin and would thus disqualify Jesus from being the sinner's Savior. Ambitions make us vulnerable to temptation. The Israelites were enticed by the power promised by the religions of the people that surrounded them. Samuel warned them to "rid yourselves of the foreign gods and the Ashtoreths and commit yourselves to

the LORD and serve him only" (1 Samuel 7:3). Sennacherib of Assyria tempted Hezekiah with military provisions if Israel joined forces with their enemy. Isaiah the prophet told Hezekiah that the power of the Lord was greater than any power Sennacherib could offer (2 Kings 18:23; 19:6, 7). The Jewish power structure offered the apostles freedom from persecution if they obeyed the will of the Sanhedrin, but Peter refused (Acts 5:27-29).

BIBLE**TRUTH** 3

Satan manipulates our fears to lead us into sin. LUKE 4:9-13

■ **In what ways is being a Christian risky? How have your fears kept you from doing the right thing sometimes?**

INSIDE STORY: Rabbinical tradition taught that the Messiah would appear on top of the temple to reveal himself to the nation. Satan challenged Jesus to prove his divinity by jumping. Such an act would capture the attention of the crowds and virtually remove the possibility that Jesus would be crucified. Jesus countered Satan's lie by quoting once again from God's Word (Deuteronomy 6:16). Jesus knew that it was wrong to take an *easy* path instead of counting on God to give strength for taking the *right* path.

It is easy to let our fears keep us from being faithful to God's plan for us. God knows this. The command, "Do not be afraid," appears almost *one hundred times* in Scripture! When Abram was afraid that he would die childless and was tempted to find another heir, God said it (Genesis 15:1-5). When King Jehoshaphat and his subjects saw their enemies surrounding them, God said it (2 Chronicles 20:2, 14, 15). When Joseph was afraid of the embarrassment he would suffer when he married a pregnant woman, God said it (Matthew 1:18-20).

CHALLENGE Have the class look up the word *temptation* in a concordance. List some of the verses and challenge students to commit one to memory this week.

THE BIG TRUTH

ANGELS ARE REAL AND HAVE IMPORTANT JOBS TO DO.

CONFIDENTIAL SOURCE:
HEBREWS 1:14;
DANIEL 4:13;
PSALM 148:2–5

Tagged

This may sound like part of some futuristic sci-fi movie, but it is, in fact, reality. Our government allows a type of microchip with radio frequency identification (RFID) to be implanted in humans.

RFID technology has been used for years. An RFID device sends off radio waves that can be picked up by computer readers. Instantly, a computer can find out where the device is, and other information embedded in the tag can be read. RFID tags have been used for years to track livestock or lost pets. But now RFID is becoming widespread as more uses are being developed.

An elementary school in Tokyo devised RFID tags to go in students' backpacks. As students pass through the school's front gate, the tags signal that the students have arrived. In just moments, parents receive e-mails indicating the exact times their children got to school. Unlike bar codes or other devices, RFID is so specific that each tag has its own identity. Therefore each student can be tracked individually. This is especially important to Japanese parents. Kidnapping is a problem there, and Japanese children often travel as long as two hours by bus or train to get to school.

Where else are RFID devices being used? Michelin puts them on tires to track products on vehicles; prisons put them on prisoners' armbands to follow their moves; Florida theme parks offer wristbands for children in case they are separated from their parents; Wal-Mart requires all merchandise sold in their stores to have the tags so inventory can be better managed; drivers in some countries have them to speed through toll booths and pay later. In the future, RFID tags could be on cell phones so people can purchase items, on prescription drugs to prevent illegal trafficking, and on passports and drivers' licenses.

But back to the implanted microchip idea. What's its purpose? The medical industry says with implants, they could better facilitate health care and track patients' medical histories. They say this could be especially beneficial if a patient is unconscious during a trauma and needs to be treated immediately. A nightclub in Spain offers implants so customers may charge their drink purchases without carrying money. Mexico is using implants in their attorney general's office to allow authorized employees access to areas in the building that contain private documents. The big question will arise as the implanted chip is developed—how can people benefit from this technology, yet keep their privacy?

QUESTIONS TO CONSIDER:

■ What do you think about this radio frequency technology? What are the benefits? What are the dangers? Would you get a microchip implant? Explain.

■ RFID tags can send information by invisible means without the user even knowing. Name some other things that work without being seen.

■ There are many things that work in this world invisibly. We read in the Bible about other invisible yet powerful forces. We cannot see angels, but God's Word assures us that they are real and working on this earth. Let's look at three duties of angels.

INSTANT STUDY 03 ■ BIBLE TRUTHS

BIBLE TRUTHS

How can we be sure that a message comes from an angel? We can't. But we *can* know whether or not any message is truly from God by comparing it to Scripture. A true angelic message would not contradict the inspired words of the Bible (Galatians 1:8).

BIBLE**TRUTH** 1

Angels serve those performing God's will on earth. HEBREWS 1:14

■ **Tell about a time when you had a problem but no one to help you with it.**

INSIDE STORY: Angels are "ministering spirits sent to serve those who will inherit salvation" (1:14). During Jesus' forty days of fasting in the wilderness, Satan tempted him, but angels came to see to his needs (Matthew 4:11). When Jesus faced his imminent arrest and crucifixion, an angel supplied him with strength (Luke 22:39-44). When Herod had marked Peter for execution, an angel appeared to orchestrate a jailbreak (Acts 12:6-10)!

Because they work invisibly, we do not know for certain how angels have been involved when we have overcome a difficult trial. But we do know that faithful, serving Christians may have "entertained angels without knowing it" (Hebrews 13:2).

BIBLE**TRUTH** 2

Angels help broadcast God's message. DANIEL 4:13

■ **A lot of people claim to talk for God. How do we know whom to believe?**

INSIDE STORY: More than a dozen people in the Bible received a message from God through an angel. Angels came to Lot to warn him about the impending destruction of Sodom (Genesis 19:1, 12, 13). An angel spoke to Philip, directing him to go to a place where he would meet a court official from Ethiopia (Acts 8:26). A specific angel, Gabriel, appeared to Mary to announce that Mary would give birth to the Messiah (Luke 1:26-38). In a dream an angel told Joseph that Mary would give birth to the Messiah (Matthew 1:18-24).

BIBLE**TRUTH** 3

Angels praise God in the courts of Heaven. PSALM 148:2-5

■ **Angels are often pictured with harps or trumpets. What's that all about?**

INSIDE STORY: Angels praise God for being a creating God (Psalm 148:5). Angels also praise God when evil is defeated. Near the end of his life, Moses sang a song about God's justice to the people of Israel (Deuteronomy 32:43). Some ancient manuscripts include a mention of angels worshiping when this takes place. In the book of Revelation we see this repeated often. (See Revelation 18.) Finally, angels praise God when people turn to him. "There is rejoicing in the presence of the angels of God over one sinner who repents" (Luke 15:10). "You have come to thousands upon thousands of angels in joyful assembly" (Hebrews 12:22).

CHALLENGE Sing the hymn, "Holy, Holy, Holy." Keep this song in mind this week as you strive to serve God and praise his holiness as the angels do.

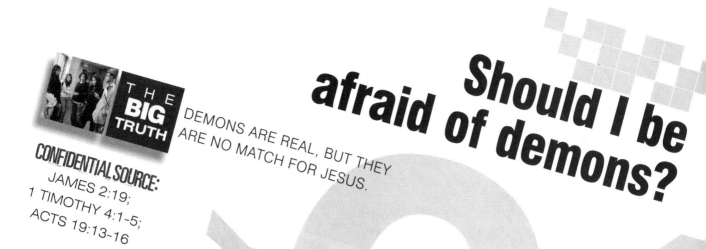

DEMONS ARE REAL, BUT THEY ARE NO MATCH FOR JESUS.

Should I be afraid of demons?

Taking a Byte Out of Evil

The Internet has been used for all sorts of wicked practices (besides the good you can find online). Nevertheless, one of the Web's leading companies continues to promise *not* to be a part of the problem. On the last day of the Web 2.0 Summit in San Francisco, a panel of former Google employees assured the audience that the company takes its "don't be evil" philosophy very seriously.

The panel confirmed to moderator and conference chair John Battelle that Google founders Larry Page and Sergey Brin consider whether or not an action will have evil consequences when making business decisions. One panel member recalled that the issue of evil was often a part of the negotiations when deciding which companies to acquire. Page and Brin would ask hard questions about the deals if they sensed that the management of a company had an evil intent. Another panel member who was once involved in product development told how the founders of Google helped employees think creatively while reminding them always to keep in mind the question of evil.

Google has long been famous for its unofficial motto, "Don't be evil." In July of 2001, about a dozen of the company's first employees met to list Google's core values. The group listed typical workplace rules like "Treat everyone with respect" and "Be on time for meetings." Finally an engineer in the group said, "All of these things can be covered by just saying, 'Don't be evil.'" The motto stuck and remains a part of the corporate philosophy page of Google's Web site.

One test of this motto took place several years ago. The Chinese government refused to allow its citizens access to Google unless certain topics sensitive to the government were blocked by the search engine. "We concluded that although we weren't wild about the restrictions, it was even worse to not try to serve those users at all," Google CEO Eric Schmidt said. "We actually did an evil scale and decided not to serve at all was worse evil," he said.

QUESTIONS TO CONSIDER:

■ What is your reaction to Google's three-word motto? According to the article, how has it shaped decision making in the company?

■ How do you define *evil*? What are some evil things? What might an evil corporation do? Who are some evildoers? List some characteristics you would expect to find in an evildoer.

■ A company like Google can claim to avoid evil and evildoers. But how well do they do that? We can name a lot of villains and evildoers. But it may be hard to clearly define *evil* and determine the source of evil. Yet the Bible helps clarify the issue by discussing evildoers of the spiritual realm— demons. God wants us to know three important characteristics of demons.

BIBLE TRUTHS

BIBLE**TRUTH** 1

Demons know that they are less powerful than God. JAMES 2:19

■ **What might be some differences between having faith in God and just admitting that he exists?**

INSIDE STORY: Most Bible scholars believe that demons were angels who rebelled against God (Jude 6). Therefore, having been created by God to be holy servants and abide with him in the heavenly places before the beginning of time, demons know there is but one God. He is the one they rose up against, and he is the one who thwarted their scheme, expelling them from glory. As a result, demons tremble at the thought of him (James 2:19). Their fear is evidence of their belief. Yet theirs is a belief that cannot save, because it is based purely on fact and not on conviction or devotion. Saving faith requires more than the knowledge of biblical truth. It calls for a personal knowledge of God that expresses itself outwardly in a changed life.

BIBLE**TRUTH** 2

Demons deceive people into believing false doctrine. 1 TIMOTHY 4:1-5

■ **Is one religion just as true as any other religion? What do you think and why?**

INSIDE STORY: A counterfeiter's goal is to produce an artificial item that is so close to the original that few people can tell the difference. Satan and his demons use a similar tactic. They distort the truth of God's Word to create a false gospel (Galatians 1:6, 7). These "things taught by demons" (1 Timothy 4:1) usually have some root in the true gospel in order to make them more believable. Tragically, those who embrace such teachings often cannot see their error because their hearts have been turned against the truth. Paul gives two examples of this. The first concerns marriage. God instituted marriage to alleviate man's loneliness and to make him whole (Genesis 2:18). Satan's demons had convinced some believers that the spiritually mature should refrain

from marriage. The second example concerns Jewish law and the acceptability of certain foods. The law declared certain foods unclean, but these prohibitions were nullified at the cross (Colossians 2:13-16). To be bound to these regulations under the new covenant is to seek salvation through works, not faith. It is the practice of demons to take elements of truth such as these and to distort them in order to lead people away from God.

BIBLE**TRUTH** 3

Demons have power over those who try to defeat them by their strength alone. ACTS 19:13-16

■ **List some ways that people fail to take the existence of evil seriously. What are some results of such beliefs if taken to extremes?**

INSIDE STORY: As Paul preached in Ephesus, the Holy Spirit validated his ministry with miracles. Mimicking Paul's work, a group of brothers attempted to cast out demons by invoking the name of Jesus but without a personal belief in him. In a confrontation with one demon-possessed man, the evil spirit acknowledged Jesus and Paul but not the brothers. The demon-possessed man then jumped on the would-be exorcists and beat them severely (Acts 19:13-16). The Bible clearly portrays demons as spiritual beings who are real, able to speak, and possessed of their own identities. Jesus acknowledged the reality of demonic influence and possession and offered instructions to his disciples about confronting evil spirits (Mark 9:14-17, 28, 29).

CHALLENGE

Distribute construction paper and have your students make a collage that includes words and/or pictures that describe some ways they are deceived by evil. Then they should include words and/or pictures that demonstrate God's victory over evil and the ways they plan to depend on Jesus to overcome evil.

Am I helpless against evil?

Fighting Fire

A few years ago, wildfires devastated parts of Southern California. The California Office of Emergency Services revealed that over 2,000 homes were destroyed. The fires, fueled by dry winds that gusted up to one hundred miles per hour, were deadly and devastating. Yet brave men and women fought the flames and provided for those affected by the flames. Here are some of those involved in the response and rescue efforts.

The American Red Cross—The Red Cross had 3,352 disaster workers in California. Twenty-four emergency shelters for fire victims were open at this time. Forty trailers filled with cots, blankets, and comfort kits supplied these shelters. About seventy-five mobile feeding trucks serviced the affected areas. A few weeks later, the Red Cross returned with cleanup supplies such as rakes, work gloves, shovels, and trash bags.

The United States Military—Over 1,500 National Guard personnel were directly engaged in immediate response to the fires. In addition, 550 active-duty Marines and 17,301 California National Guardsmen were available to be called as needed. A total of fourteen helicopters from the National Guard, U.S. Navy, and Marine Corps fought the fire from the air. The United States Coast Guard provided aircraft to help move cargo and additional government personnel into affected areas.

Other Federal Agencies—Because of the widespread damage caused by the many fires in Southern California and the threat to public safety, the United States Department of Agriculture (USDA) Forest Service closed the San Bernardino, Angeles, Cleveland, and Los Padres National Forests. The USDA's Food & Nutrition Service Regional Office worked with California to implement a Disaster Food Stamp Program and to make other plans for feeding disaster victims.

Animal Protection Agencies—At Fiesta Island in Mission Bay, San Diego a shelter for pets and livestock was set up. One hundred and forty horses, more than one hundred dogs, thirty-five goats, and some cats and birds were sheltered there and cared for by their owners. Hay and animal food was provided by animal services. Petsmart® charities sent two tractor-trailers stocked with supplies for pets. Each "Emergency Relief Waggin'" trailer contained enough pet products, food, and supplies to support up to 500 animals.

QUESTIONS TO CONSIDER:

■ Review the number of people and variety of tasks that were done in response to the California wildfires. What about them surprises you? What necessary services in response to this disaster would you have not thought about?

■ Consider difficult tasks that you are called to perform. How are you equipped to perform them? What people are necessary to help you with them?

■ Many people were equipped to fight the fires of California and their results. God tells us in the Bible that he wants to equip us to fight an even more devastating fire and the results of it—the fire of Hell and the wrath of Satan. Let's discover more about this spiritual warfare.

BIBLE TRUTHS

BIBLE**TRUTH** 1

God shapes our behavior to protect us from attack. EPHESIANS 6:14

■ **How would you feel if a Christian leader you respected was involved in serious sin? How does having good character protect us?**

INSIDE STORY: Paul compared the tools God gives Christians to battle evil to the armor the typical Roman soldier wore. When Paul wrote these words, he was chained and guarded by a soldier (Acts 28:16-20)! The first piece of armor the soldier wore was a broad leather belt that gathered the soldier's tunic and kept him from tripping in battle. Truth is our belt. We do not beat the devil using his key weapons—lies. Having a reputation for truth keeps us from getting "tripped up" with a reputation for dishonesty.

The Roman soldier put on a breastplate to guard his vital organs when battle became quick, close, and personal. Paul compared righteousness to that breastplate. When we live and work in proximity to unbelievers, they may try to refute our testimony about Christ by revealing our darkest sins. When we live righteous lives, those attacks just bounce off our armor and are disregarded as "ignorant talk of foolish men" (1 Peter 2:15).

BIBLE**TRUTH** 2

God unites us with other Christians to join us in battle. EPHESIANS 6:15, 16

■ **Tell about a task that was impossible for you to accomplish without help. Why might spiritual warfare be like that?**

INSIDE STORY: Roman soldiers wore low half boots so they could march rapidly and stand firm in battle with other soldiers. The Christian marches and stands on the gospel of peace. We are called to be prepared to defend our faith (1 Peter 3:15). The early church all wore the same "shoes" because they "devoted themselves to the apostles' teaching and to the fellowship" (Acts 2:42). Corporate worship and study is a must for us today as well.

Roman shields could lock together, forming a wall of protection for a battalion. The Christian's shield is faith. The onslaught of the devil's fiery arrows—despair, doubt, depression—can be extinguished by the united faith of the church. Faith is not just a personal matter, but also a vital part of "the salvation we share" as we "contend for the faith" as a community (Jude 3).

BIBLE**TRUTH** 3

God gives us protection and weaponry that are invincible. EPHESIANS 6:17, 18

■ **List some of the most effective weapons of modern warfare. Why are they so effective?**

INSIDE STORY: The Roman soldier's helmet was made of bronze, protecting him from a deadly blow to the head. Christians wear a helmet of salvation. Even death is not fatal! We have eternal life in Heaven. As Paul had previously written to the Romans, when we are securely fixed in God's care, live or die, we win (Romans 8:35-39).

The Roman's weapon was a short-blade sword, designed for close-up, man-to-man fighting. The Christian's weapon is the Spirit's sword, the Word of God. This is the same weapon Jesus used against the devil (Matthew 4:1-11). The Word of God is a powerful weapon (Hebrews 4:12) and is the one by which our returning Savior will conquer (Revelation 19:11-16). On top of the six pieces of armor, one more thing is necessary: prayer. Like any good soldier we must always "be alert" and stand on guard for our fellow soldiers as we "keep on praying" for them (Ephesians 6:18). To use a modern image, prayer is our radio contact with headquarters.

CHALLENGE Consider having a commitment ceremony in which your students are "knighted" as they prepare to put on their armor and engage in spiritual warfare.

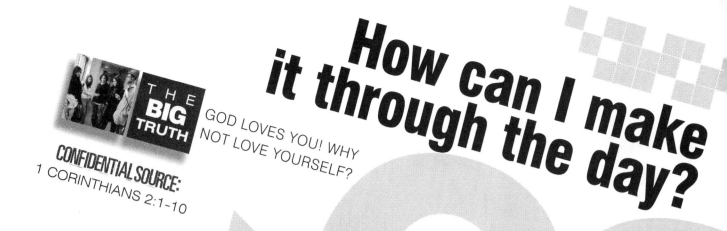

How can I make it through the day?

Lite-Brite Idea

Mark Beekman liked playing with his Lite-Brite toy as a kid. But as an adult, he decided to use Lite-Brite pegs to make art—a replica of Leonardo DaVinci's "Last Supper" painting. The resulting piece measured about five feet high and ten feet wide and earned him a Guinness World Record. The "World's Largest Lite-Brite" sold on eBay for $15,000, with the money going to a charity that helps children who are orphaned.

Where did Mark get his big idea? He said, "I was looking into building a Lego mosaic originally," but felt that it had been done many times. Instead, he chose Lite-Brite pegs—124,418 pegs, to be exact! First he built a "canvas" with sheet metal. Then he had to purchase enough pegs. He ordered 100,000 pegs directly from Hasbro, the company that makes the toy. "Once I ran out of those, I had to buy every single Lite-Brite in every single store in a 15-mile radius just over and over and over," Mark said.

Then Mark had another hurdle to jump, as described on his MySpace page: "An actual Lite-Brite toy has a black background which utilizes blank spaces as black, but does not have black pegs. For artistic and Guinness World Record purposes, I was unable to leave blank spaces. What to do? Unused pegs were painted black . . ."

Finally, Mark tried to be disciplined at putting in two rows of pegs a day, which took a bit of time. In fact, making his big idea come to life was a lot of hard work. "I just kind of put it in my head that it had to be done, so I just made myself do it," Mark said.

Another reason motivated Mark in his project—making unusual art that could be relevant to all ages. "When I was a kid, you couldn't have paid me to go to an art museum. I thought art was boring. With this piece, I wanted to appeal to kids as well as the kid in all of us. I want people to realize that art is whatever they want it to be. It doesn't have to fit a category, and it certainly doesn't have to be boring."

Mark said that he's satisfied with his creation. "I'm very happy with how it turned out. There are always little imperfections and, you know, it's my baby. So I'm nitpicking over the details. But everyone who sees it is pretty much overwhelmed."

QUESTIONS
TO CONSIDER:

■ Did you play with a Lite-Brite toy as a kid? What pictures did you like to make with it? Why do you think creative activities make us feel good about ourselves?

■ How do you think Mark Beekman felt after he accomplished something he worked so hard to do? From his words in the article, why do you think Mark is confident in his achievement?

■ Achieving a goal can give us confidence. Think about your proudest accomplishment. How did accomplishing the feat make you more confident? What other things make you feel confident on a day-to-day basis? On the other hand, how does failing to meet a goal affect your confidence? What things make you feel insecure?

■ We all have days when we feel better about ourselves than others. But must our self-confidence always be tied to what we accomplish? The apostle Paul gives different reasons for his confidence.

INSTANT STUDY 06 ■ BIBLETRUTHS

BIBLE TRUTHS

BIBLE**TRUTH** 1

Paul was confident because of who he knew, not what he knew. 1 CORINTHIANS 2:1, 2

■ **Can there be such a thing as a "Christian superstar?" Why or why not?**

INSIDE STORY: Paul reminded the Corinthians that he did not come to them with superior speech or knowledge (1 Corinthians 2:1). Many people attempt to derive their self-esteem from what they know. True confidence comes only from a right relationship with God. When Paul came to Corinth during his second missionary journey, he did not take up residence as a prestigious visiting rabbi. Rather, he earned a living as a tradesman. He lived with tentmakers Pricilla and Aquila and worked with them (Acts 18:1-3).

Paul wanted to do one thing in Corinth—to present Jesus Christ and his sacrifice (1 Corinthians 2:2). The Corinthians surely remembered Paul's early days in their city. Sabbath after Sabbath, Paul "reasoned in the synagogue, trying to persuade Jews and Greeks" that Jesus was the promised Messiah (Acts 18:4).

BIBLE**TRUTH** 2

Paul was confident because of who used his words, not the words he used. 1 CORINTHIANS 2:3-5

■ **Tell about a time when you talked your way out of trouble.**

INSIDE STORY: Some people are confident because they can "talk their way out of anything." The opposite was true with Paul. In Corinth, he put himself in positions that he couldn't talk his way out of. He infuriated the religious establishment by literally shaking the dust off his clothes at them (Acts 18:6)! Furthermore, he boldly continued to preach in a house that was just next door to the synagogue of Jews he offended (v. 7). No wonder Paul preached "with much trembling" (1 Corinthians 2:3)! One can only imagine the tension that existed.

But rather than relying on his words, he relied on God to use his words "with a demonstration of the Spirit's power" (v. 4). This demonstration came. Though Paul refused to use a slick patter and glib arguments to convince people to join him, God empowered his preaching and made it successful. Even in that stressful environment, Crispus, the leader of the synagogue that opposed Paul, became a Christian along with the rest of his household. Many more Corinthians also believed and were baptized (Acts 18:8).

BIBLE**TRUTH** 3

Paul was confident because his message was from a majority of one, not one of the majority. 1 CORINTHIANS 2:6-10

■ **What is meant by the adage, "There is strength in numbers"? Is it always true? Explain.**

INSIDE STORY: Being different can make one a target. Therefore, people may have confidence because they act and think the same as those surrounding them. But Paul refused to play along and to speak "the wisdom of this age or of the rulers of this age" (v. 6). No matter what the other scholars were teaching, Paul was committed to "God's secret wisdom" (v. 7). When in Corinth, Paul knew that this approach made him vulnerable. But God promised him in a dream that he would be protected (Acts 18:9, 10). Even when his enemies took him to court, Paul was unfazed. God's promise was kept, and his case before the Roman proconsul Gallio was dismissed (vv. 12-17).

CHALLENGE If they are available this time of year, buy a bag of Valentine conversation hearts candy. Have students imagine that the messages on the hearts are from God to them. Have each student pick out one particular message to take home, reminding him or her to be confident in God's love.

INSTANT **STUDY** 06 . . . CONTINUED

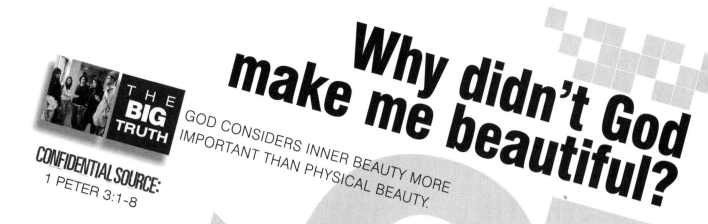

Why didn't God make me beautiful?

THE BIG TRUTH

CONFIDENTIAL SOURCE:
1 PETER 3:1-8

GOD CONSIDERS INNER BEAUTY MORE IMPORTANT THAN PHYSICAL BEAUTY.

Hollywood Beauty

What makes people beautiful? A few news stories share some of society's prevalent views.

Something's fishy—How do glamorous celebrities seek to keep their beauty? Their secret is caviar, or more specifically a cream made from the eggs of the Baerii sturgeon, reared on farms in the south of France. The treatment costs just under $400.

Angelina Jolie admits using such a treatment. Jolie became worried because the veins on her arms, hands, and forehead became more visible after she lost some weight. Gwyneth Paltrow, Rolling Stones star Mick Jagger, supermodel Kate Moss, and fashion designer Stella McCartney are all said to be fans of caviar-based facial treatments.

Pirate queen—*Pirates of the Caribbean* star Keira Knightley topped a United Kingdom poll and was named the beauty icon of 2007. The results of the poll, taken by British health and beauty chain Superdrug, contained all British celebrities with the exception of U.S. citizen Paris Hilton.

Superdrug's beauty director, Katherine Le Clerc, said: "The top 10 beauty icons list shows that today there is room for everyone's idea of true beauty . . . from the aloof glamour of Keira Knightley and Victoria (Posh Spice of the Spice Girls) Beckham's high-maintenance gloss to the fresh faced youthful looks of (British TV hostesses) Fearne Cotton [and] Holly Willoughby and (fashion model) Gemma Atkinson."

Back by unpopular demand—When a TV writer's strike and holiday reruns limited TV choices, some viewers tuned to the CW TV network in search for original programming. Apparently, this was enough to convince producers of the self-proclaimed "mother of all beauty pageants" to begin work on a second season. *Crowned*, a reality show in which mother-daughter teams compete in a twisted beauty pageant quickly began auditioning contestants for *Crowned 2*.

The audition notice promised a $100,000 prize and "a fabulous pair of tiaras" to the eventual winners. *Crowned* garnered a moderate audience, but was panned by the critics. Gillian Flynn of *Entertainment Weekly* labeled the beauty queen hopefuls as "dismissably rotten, which makes watching them a chore." So much for the eye of the beholder . . .

QUESTIONS
TO CONSIDER:

■ Consider the ideas about beauty in the stories above. What traits or features are considered to be attractive? What traits or features are thought to be unattractive? What would you add to this list?

■ What evidence do you see that most people consider beauty to deal only with outward appearances? What inner qualities, in your opinion, also make a person beautiful? If you were to hold an "inner beauty pageant," who would some of the contestants be? Explain your choices.

■ Polls, celebrities, and TV audiences are drawn to those with physical beauty. But is this true beauty? God tells us in the Bible that there is much more to being beautiful.

BIBLE TRUTHS

BIBLE**TRUTH** 1

Beauty comes from within, not from adornment.
1 PETER 3:1-4

■ **Imagine a restaurant with very attractive waiters and waitresses but bad food. How often would you dine there? Why?**

INSIDE STORY: Believing women in Peter's day wanted to win their unbelieving spouses to Christ. Preaching to them only seemed to make the problem worse. Peter asserted that these husbands could be won by the godly behavior of their wives (v. 1). For that reason, Peter advised that women not be obsessed with "outward adornment, such as braided hair and the wearing of gold jewelry and fine clothes." True beauty is internal, the "unfading beauty of a gentle and quiet spirit" (vv. 3, 4).

Titus ministered in Crete, an island known for its low moral standards (Titus 1:12). Paul taught him that the best way to have the gospel be noticed in such a culture is to allow the work of the Spirit to be evident in the lives of believers (2:6-8). Even overlooked slaves would "make the teaching about God our Savior attractive" by their transformed behavior (vv. 9, 10). The beauty of a changed character allows God's light to "shine before men," lending credibility to the gospel (Matthew 5:16).

BIBLE**TRUTH** 2

Beauty lasts for all time and is not dictated by changing styles. 1 PETER 3:5, 6

■ **Think about a fashion trend that was popular ten years ago. Is it considered fashionable today? Why or why not?**

INSIDE STORY: Today's hottest fashions become ice cold in a very short period of time. On the other hand, godly character is always in style. It was that character that made women of the Old Testament truly beautiful (1 Peter 3:5). Rebekah's compassion for a weary traveler and his animals is what drew the interest of the servant who sought a wife for Isaac (Genesis 24:14-19). The courage that the prostitute

Rahab showed when protecting Israelite spies—not her jewelry or wardrobe—is what is remembered yet today (Joshua 2:2-4). Ruth remained loyal to her mother-in-law, and her profession of that devotion is just as beautiful today as it was centuries ago (Ruth 1:16-18). In all of those cases, godly character meant taking risks. Placing one's life in the hands of another is always frightening. But when such fear is overcome, true beauty shines (1 Peter 3:6).

BIBLE**TRUTH** 3

Beauty is found in relationships, not glamorous individuals. 1 PETER 3:7, 8

■ **Think of a good friend. How does that friendship make you a better person?**

INSIDE STORY: A cultural view of beauty imagines that all eyes in the room turn to a beautiful person who enters. But true beauty makes others feel valued, not inferior. God's goal is not that individual Christians have beautiful bodies. God's goal is that individual Christians be joined by his Spirit to *become* one beautiful body, the body of Christ (Romans 12:4-21). We are called to "live in harmony with one another," displaying relationship-building characteristics of sympathy, love, compassion, and humility (1 Peter 3:8).

Peter implied that a man's relationship with God is affected negatively when he mistreats his wife (1 Peter 3:7). This idea is echoed elsewhere in the Bible. Jesus told his disciples to compare God's ability to forgive them with their ability to forgive others (Matthew 6:12). John told Christians that hatred of other Christians blinded them and kept them from knowing the path God wanted them to take in life (1 John 2:9-11).

CHALLENGE Help your class nominate contestants for an inner beauty pageant. For each nomination reasons should be given why that person demonstrates an inner, godly beauty.

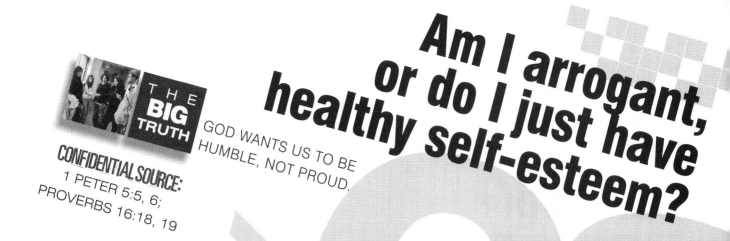

CONFIDENTIAL SOURCE:
1 PETER 5:5, 6;
PROVERBS 16:18, 19

GOD WANTS US TO BE
HUMBLE, NOT PROUD.

Am I arrogant, or do I just have healthy self-esteem?

Road Hazards

There is something about being in a car that seems to magnify self-centeredness. Here are some examples.

Life in the fast lane—An unnamed eighty-five-year-old motorist lost his license and his Oldsmobile for a week. He also faced a hefty fine after becoming the oldest person arrested for violating an Ontario law aimed at cracking down on street racers. Although the roads were snow and ice-covered, the man was clocked traveling at one hundred miles per hour, forty miles per hour over speed limit. Under the new law, drivers who exceed the speed limit by thirty-one miles per hour or more can lose both their vehicle and license for one week, along with a fine of at least $2,002. "He said he was going to the bank and shopping," said Ontario Provincial Police Sergeant Cam Woolley. Most of those charged under the new speed law have been men in their mid-twenties to mid-thirties, but at least twenty drivers aged sixty-five and older, including three women, have been charged.

Life in the slow lane—An English woman was banned from driving for seven days after traveling at speeds of less than ten miles per hour on the highway near Bristol, England. Fifty-eight-year-old Stephanie Cole straddled the hard shoulder and inside lane as she dawdled along a stretch of highway near her home. In the back window of the car was a sign that said: "I don't do fast; please overtake." Cole admitted driving without reasonable consideration and was told she would have to take another driving test at the end of the ban.

Lane in the high life—Honduran foreign minister Milton Jimenez resigned after local television aired a video that caught him punching police after he was arrested for drunk driving. Jimenez, a close aide of President Manuel Zelaya, was arrested and taken to a police station, where he ended up in a fistfight with police officers. A local television channel broadcast the cell phone-taped video.

Bike on the pain lane—Police said they arrested a man who admitted digging holes on a park bike trail. Warren John Wilson did so because he was nearly run down by a cyclist. Sergeant Linda King said that nearly fifty holes measuring about one foot by two feet had been found along a trail at Laguna Lake Park in California, and in some cases attempts had been made to hide them from cyclists. She said some riders went over their handlebars after hitting the holes, but none reported major injuries.

QUESTIONS TO CONSIDER:

■ Some might describe the people mentioned in the article above as *arrogant*. What actions might lead one to make such a description? What dangers to other drivers do arrogant drivers cause?

■ Without naming names, describe arrogant actions of people other than drivers. Have you ever done something that might have caused others to describe you as being arrogant? Tell about it.

■ Some people take to the road with an attitude that they are more important than others. But arrogance is an easy thing to develop, on or off the road. The cure for arrogance, the trait of humility, takes work to obtain. Let's look at what God says about choosing humility.

BIBLE **TRUTH** 1

Pride uses blessings to achieve personal comfort and power. PROVERBS 16:18, 19

■ **List some ways that pride differs from confidence.**

INSIDE STORY: Adam and Eve attempted to become like God, separating themselves from God's grace (Genesis 3). Solomon echoes that truth saying, "Pride goes before destruction" (Proverbs 16:18). Other verses in Proverbs declare that pride is an evil to be hated, leads to disgrace, and breeds quarrels (8:13; 11:2; 13:10). The arrogant are humiliated when their pretensions overreach their true status. They may suffer public embarrassment in this life and certainly will go down to destruction in the life to come.

Peter was chosen by Jesus to follow and learn from him. But distortion of that privilege turned to pride. By the time he had spent most of three years following Jesus, Peter boldly promised, "Even if all fall away, I will not. . . . Even if I have to die with you, I will never disown you" (Mark 14:29 31). But a few hours later that same night Peter denied Jesus three times. Thirty years later, as a respected apostle and leader, Peter remembered his own pride in his younger days. Aiming his words first to young men, Peter said, "Be submissive to those who are older" (1 Peter 5:5). He used a term that was often found in a military context, where it meant "put yourself under the authority of" a superior officer. (The same word was used by Paul in Romans 13:1, where he told Christians to "submit" themselves to the authorities in their government.) As Peter himself finally had learned, if we want to follow in the steps of Jesus, we have to learn that neither our nature nor our position is a license to feel superior to others.

BIBLE **TRUTH** 2

Humility uses blessings selflessly. 1 PETER 5:5, 6

■ **Why might pride stand in the way of worshiping God?**

INSIDE STORY: Humble people rejoice in what God has made them and find their worth in being his children. This leads to a healthy relationship with God. God loves humility.

He "takes delight" in his people; he "crowns the humble with salvation" (Psalm 149:4). Though proud and wicked people have no room for God in their hearts (Psalm l0:4), humble people are glad to embrace God and accept his help. More importantly, God is glad to embrace them! Peter had heard Jesus himself say, "Everyone who exalts himself will be humbled, and he who humbles himself will be exalted" (Luke 14:11). He also recalled the words of Solomon in Proverbs 3:34, "God opposes the proud but gives grace to the humble" (1 Peter 5:5). When people are full of pride, they become rivals with God for the right to sit on the throne of their lives. On the other hand, when people humble themselves they are in a position to receive God's grace (1 Peter 5:6).

Humility also leads to a healthy relationship with other people. When we recognize that who we are is a gift of God, we are more likely to see God's goodness in others. Counseling humility for all Christians, Peter commanded, "clothe yourselves with humility toward one another" (1 Peter 5:5). Compare the similar statement of Paul, "Submit to one another out of reverence for Christ" (Ephesians 5:21).

Both Greek and Roman writers confined humility to slaves and low-class people. People who could hold their heads high in society did not need to debase themselves by practicing humility. But society's way is not God's way. Since value comes from God alone, we are free to embrace others regardless of social or economic status (Proverbs 16:19).

CHALLENGE

Help the class list some simple acts of humility that they can easily practice next week. Some examples include: At the store, let someone go in front of you in line. When you work on a group project at school, give your partners credit for their work by complimenting their efforts to your teacher. Do a few extra chores around the house without being asked and without telling anyone that you did them. Spend a day with your friends and listen to their problems without ever mentioning any of yours.

WE ARE NOT NUMBER ONE!

CONFIDENTIAL SOURCE:
PHILIPPIANS 2:4;
PSALM 112:5; ACTS 20:35

What is my responsibility to others?

Dangerous Appetites

Because bald eagles are protected under federal law, it's a crime to kill them. Nevertheless, more than twenty of the protected birds died in Alaska a few years ago. The birds were not victims of poachers or hunters, but of their own appetites.

On a cold winter day, a truck driver parked his vehicle outside of the Ocean Beauty Seafoods plant in Kodiak, Alaska. Unfortunately he did not secure the vehicle's retractable fabric cover. This left his cargo, tons of fish guts, open to the elements for just a few minutes.

Within that short time period, around fifty bald eagles swarmed upon the truck, enticed by its tasty payload. Nineteen eagles were crushed to death by the rest of the hungry horde. Some of the birds became so covered in their gooey feast that they exhausted themselves trying to fly away after gorging themselves.

With temperatures in the mid-teens, many of the eagles began to succumb to the cold.

Brandon Saito, a biologist with the U.S. Fish and Wildlife Service, coordinated an opportunity to rescue the greedy birds. The rescue team dumped the truck's contents onto the floor of the Ocean Beauty plant to rescue the eagles still caught in the muck.

The eagles were then cleaned with dish soap in tubs of warm water to remove the oily slime and warm them. The survivors were taken to a heated fish and wildlife warehouse to recover—some of them in critical condition. Saito said they would be released as soon as they were dry and strong enough.

There was a concern that some birds would have to be sent to Anchorage for further treatment at the Bird Treatment and Learning Center, but most appeared to be doing well the next day. Gary Wheeler, manager of the Kodiak National Wildlife Refuge, reported, "We were pleasantly surprised this morning that the vast majority of the birds perked up overnight."

QUESTIONS TO CONSIDER:

■ While the above story may seem trivial, how does it illustrate the danger of being driven by appetite alone? What caused the death of all of these eagles? How could the incident have been prevented? Are the eagles themselves to blame, or is it the fault of others? Defend your answer.

■ People differ from animals in that our ability to reason can be used to override our greed. But does this always happen? Give some examples when a person's selfish appetites brought about disastrous consequences for him or her. When has your own selfishness brought trouble to you?

■ Selfishness caused the death of these noble birds. But eagles, as beautiful as they are, cannot help but be motivated by their desires alone. On the other hand, human beings have a choice. Too often, however, people choose to be selfish rather than generous, bringing trouble to themselves. The Bible tells us to choose generosity over selfishness. Let's examine how we can avoid the fate of these eagles and become people who look out for others and not just ourselves.

BIBLE TRUTHS

BIBLE**TRUTH** 1

God gives us enough to share. PHILIPPIANS 2:4

■ **Define** *ambition*. **What is good about it? On the other hand, how can it make us blind to the needs of others?**

INSIDE STORY: When Paul was imprisoned in Rome, the Philippians probably began to fear for their own safety. Time to look out for number one! In response to that thinking, Paul urged them to have the kind of attitude that is not self-centered. Because Christians share the same love, spirit, and purpose, Paul told them to do nothing out of selfish ambition or empty conceit (vv. 2, 3). Being secure in their position as beloved children of God, they were to exercise humility and consider others as more important than themselves.

Paul summed up his challenge with these words: "Each of you should look not only to your own interests, but also to the interests of others" (Philippians 2:4). Note the wisdom in this two-part statement. Paul affirms that acting in one's own self-interest is appropriate; it is part of a God-given instinct for self-preservation. Yet he continues with another command. Christians must care about the well being of others.

BIBLE**TRUTH** 2

Blessings come from God's abundance. PSALM 112:5

■ **What are some natural resources that are limited in supply? On the other hand, name some renewable resources.**

INSIDE STORY: A common assumption is that economics is a "zero sum game." In other words, when one person has wealth, he must have taken it from someone else. When someone gives goods away, he takes a smaller slice of the economic pie so someone else may have a fair share. An ancient psalm gives another view. A person is not blessed materially because he takes from those who do not have. Rather, the man "who is generous and lends freely" will receive even more goodness (v. 5).

"Wealth and riches are in his house," even though "he has scattered abroad his gifts to the poor" (vv. 3, 9). The Bible talks about wealth built by generosity.

The reason for this distinction is a proper understanding of the source of wealth. The amount of blessings is not fixed but comes from God's unlimited supply. That is why God challenged those who refused to tithe out of fear of giving away what they might need (Malachi 3:10).

BIBLE**TRUTH** 3

God's faithful servants have set an example of generosity for others to follow. ACTS 20:35

■ **Name the most generous person you know. List some other traits of that person. How are those traits linked to generosity?**

INSIDE STORY: At the end of his third missionary journey, Paul called for the elders from the church in Ephesus to meet him in nearby Miletus. Paul reminded them how he had brought them the gospel at great personal risk and did not hesitate to proclaim to them the whole will of God (Acts 20:17-27). He urged these elders to follow his example in being selfless shepherds of the flock. Sacrifice from leaders would be necessary to protect the church from false teachers (vv. 28-31). Like Paul they should work hard to help the weak (v. 35).

Most of all they were to remember a saying of Jesus, which Paul himself had taught them: "It is more blessed to give than to receive" (v. 35). These precise words of Jesus are not recorded anywhere in the four Gospels, but the overall principle fills his sermons and is the theme of his life. Jesus "did not come to be served, but to serve, and to give his life as a ransom for many" (Mark 10:45).

CHALLENGE Read the "obituary" of Jesus in Philippians 2:5-11, telling of his selfless, serving life. Ask students to use these verses as a model to write obituaries for themselves that recount their own selfless service over the next sixty years.

Why shouldn't I just follow the crowd?

FOLLOWING THE CROWD MAY BE EASY, BUT IT IS DANGEROUS.

CONFIDENTIAL SOURCE:
EXODUS 32:1-9, 35;
PROVERBS 29:25;
ROMANS 12:2

Rat or Right?

Over the past years, a slogan became popular throughout the hip-hop music community. It appeared on T-shirts, Web sites, and even an underground DVD featuring an NBA star talking to drug dealers. Fans are told to "Stop Snitchin'."

The campaign is rooted in the idea that people should not cooperate with law enforcement authorities under any circumstances. Rappers have been quick to live by that idea. A few years ago, rap star Lil' Kim was convicted of lying to a federal grand jury to protect friends who were involved in a shootout outside a radio station. Rapper Cam'ron was a victim of a shooting and attempted robbery in Washington, DC, but refused to help the police find his assailant. Also, Busta Rhymes' bodyguard Israel Ramirez was murdered at a video shoot, but Rhymes refused to speak to the police about the matter.

Alonzo Washington, a community activist in Kansas City, sees the "Stop Snitchin'" campaign as a way of using peer pressure to promote witness intimidation. Washington finds the idea of withholding evidence that could put a murderer behind bars counterproductive. "I understand the fact that there's some problems between African-Americans and the police," he said, "[but] people have to be able to come forward."

In response to the "Stop Snitchin'" campaign, Washington released a line of T-shirts of his own design to encourage witnesses to cooperate with the police. One of the shirts Washington designed has a picture of "Omega Man," one of his comic book characters, on it. Omega Man is shown melting a snowman (a hip-hop symbol for a cocaine dealer) with a laser gun. The phone numbers for a police hotline and an image of a $100 bill is on the back of another shirt that says, "Snitch to Get Rich."

"The message is, if you don't have the goodness in your heart to turn somebody in, then do it for the money," Washington said.

QUESTIONS TO CONSIDER:

■ How do you feel about the "Stop Snitchin'" campaign? Has anyone you have known ever worn such a T-shirt? What are some reasons people feel pressured not to tell on their friends? What do you think the difference is (if any) between being a "tattle-tale" or a traitor to one's friends and helping authorities protect people?

■ Have you ever felt pressure from your peers to protect someone who did something wrong? Tell about it. What are some other examples of peer pressure you have faced? How do you usually respond to peer pressure?

■ Peer pressure is an everyday occurrence for many of us. Peer pressure is not a new phenomenon. Even people living during Bible days sometimes felt intimidated by their peers into condoning or even participating in activities that they knew were wrong.

■ Let's look at the experience of Aaron, the brother of Moses, when he faced such pressure.

BIBLE TRUTHS

BIBLE**TRUTH** 1

Aaron reacted with alarm to Moses' absence and unrest in the camp. EXODUS 32:1; PROVERBS 29:25

■ **Fear sometimes causes us to bow to peer pressure. List some consequences we fear may occur if we do not follow the crowd.**

INSIDE STORY: On Mount Sinai, God gave Moses the Ten Commandments and other laws and ordinances (Exodus 20–23). When Moses made these known to the people, again they declared, "Everything the LORD has said we will do" (24:3). Moses later went back up on the terrifying mountain and stayed there for forty days and nights (vv. 15-18). Near the end of that period, the people came to Aaron complaining about Moses' absence. They asked Aaron to create a visible image for them to follow (32:1). A brief period of apparent inactivity on God's part was used to challenge his people concerning God's clear command forbidding idolatry.

If we could have read Aaron's mind at that time, surely his thoughts would have been full of fear. What if Moses *didn't* come back? What if this nation in the wilderness decided to rebel against him forcefully? Perhaps Solomon recalled the trouble peer pressure got Aaron into when he later wrote: "Fear of man will prove to be a snare" (Proverbs 29:25). The word *fear* used here is translated "panic" elsewhere (1 Samuel 14:15). When our views run counter to the majority, it is easy to panic and begin to doubt God's presence and promises.

BIBLE**TRUTH** 2

Aaron responded by copying the practices of those around him. EXODUS 32:2-6; ROMANS 12:2

■ **Tell of someone you know who changed because he or she bowed to peer pressure. List some specific changes.**

INSIDE STORY: Aaron asked for contributions of gold jewelry and forged an idol of a calf (Exodus 32:2-4). Aaron declared that a festival would be held the following day to

honor the Lord by celebrating before this idol (vv. 5, 6). Israel had just spent years in Egypt and would have been acquainted with the Egyptian goddess Hathor. Hathor was often depicted as a golden cow and was worshiped with music and dance (see vv. 18, 19). The people of Canaan worshiped Hathor as the goddess Ashtoreth, a practice that the Israelites would adopt—to the displeasure of God (Judges 2:12, 13). The Greeks (especially in Corinth) would later worship Hathor as Aphrodite, which led to the immorality Paul condemned in his letters to the church in that city (1 Corinthians 6:18). It seems reasonable to speculate that Aaron copied one of the gods from the nation that once held him captive. We are warned, "Do not conform any longer to the pattern of this world" (Romans 12:2).

BIBLE**TRUTH** 3

Aaron led himself and others into sinful practices. EXODUS 32:7-9, 35; PROVERBS 29:25; ROMANS 12:2B

■ **Tell about a time when you later regretted succumbing to peer pressure.**

INSIDE STORY: God told Moses of the corruption of the stubborn people he declared to be his own (Exodus 32:7-9). As a result, God "struck the people with a plague" (v. 35). Peer pressure often leads to sin and its consequences. King Solomon repeats this theme. While it is enticing to follow the crowd, we must resist (Proverbs 1:10) because "a companion of fools suffers harm" (13:20). Seeking to be in the company of those who "talk about making trouble" is deadly (24:1, 2) and is like a path covered with "thorns and snares" (22:5). On the other hand, Solomon promised, "whoever trusts in the LORD is kept safe" (29:25). In the New Testament we are assured that the Holy Spirit will fight peer pressure by "the renewing of your mind" (Romans 12:2).

CHALLENGE Brainstorm with your students to list some one-line answers to peers when they attempt to lead them into ungodly behavior. (Ex: If I did that I'd be grounded for life, or Why don't we [safe activity] instead?)

Does anyone care that I'm alive?

Good Sports

The soccer field or basketball court may hold a cure for the campus blues!

With some studies showing that one in ten college students contemplate suicide, survey results published in an issue of the *Medicine and Science in Sports and Exercise Journal* hold news of interest. Using data collected from nearly five thousand college undergraduates, researchers David R. Brown and Curtis J. Blanton from the Centers for Disease Control and Prevention discovered that those who participated in team sports were statistically less likely to consider or attempt suicide.

About one out of eight men who were not on varsity or intramural teams had thoughts of suicide over the past twelve months compared to about one of fourteen men who were on athletic teams. About one out of eight women who were not on sports teams had thoughts of suicide over the past twelve months compared to about one of twelve women who were on athletic teams.

Because exercise itself is thought to ease depression, it would seem logical that suicidal thoughts would decrease for anyone who was moderately or vigorously active. Yet the study did not see a clear benefit for those who exercised but were not on a sports squad. No suicide risk reduction could be shown for men with regular solo exercise programs. Even more surprising, women who were rated as moderately or vigorously active but who were not in team sports were at greater risk for suicidal behavior.

"Team sports can provide a healing social environment," hypothesized Brown. "Being on a team, in the company of coaches and other athletes, provides a network of social support."

College years can be difficult. Students are usually miles away from home for the first time in their lives. Being separated from the support of parents and childhood friends can bring about loneliness that could lead to thoughts of suicide. It is logical that being a part of a supportive group whose members share similar goals would reduce that risk.

QUESTIONS TO CONSIDER:

■ Tell about a time when you felt lonely. What do you think caused those feelings? How did you overcome those feelings?

■ Researcher Brown stated, "Team sports can provide a healing social environment." Have you experienced that type of environment on a sports team? What other organizations have you found to provide such an environment?

■ Is there a source of support available even when no one else is present? Explain.

■ We have all experienced loneliness. Feeling separated from family and friends can be crippling. Clubs and teams are of some help, but is there another way to fight loneliness? Psalm 73:21-26 gives us three reasons for hope in the midst of loneliness.

BIBLE TRUTHS

BIBLE**TRUTH** 1

God loves us when no one else will. PSALM 73:21-23

■ **Tell about a time when the words of others made you doubt your self-worth.**

INSIDE STORY: Loneliness causes us to question our value. Note that the author of Psalm 73 understood those feelings and confronted issues of self-doubt. Describing himself as "senseless and ignorant" and as "a brute beast," the psalmist openly confessed his feelings of worthlessness (v. 22). Consider how often people use animal metaphors to denigrate a person's value: "She's such a dog." "He is a dumb ape." "What a pig!" Asaph noted that his low self-esteem left him in grief and bitterness (v. 21).

But the secret of positive self-esteem is not denying who we are. It is understanding that despite what we are, the creator of all still cares. "Yet," Asaph continued, "I am always with you" (v. 23a). In his ministry on earth, Jesus loved the unlovely. When dining at Simon the Pharisee's house, a sinful woman burst in uninvited and washed and anointed Jesus' feet. Simon assumed that Jesus did not know of the woman's shady reputation. But Jesus *did* know and loved the woman anyway (Luke 7:36-50). God sees us for who we are and yet welcomes us into his presence. He recognizes our value and is ever present, holding our hand (Psalm 73:23b).

BIBLE**TRUTH** 2

God will take us where no one else can. PSALM 73:24

■ **What plans do you have for the future? How might you feel if some of those plans do not work out?**

INSIDE STORY: Lonely people may feel "stuck"—that their lives will never change for the better. We need a relationship to give us direction and purpose. Asaph showed how God meets that need in two ways.

God directs our life on earth. "You guide me with your counsel," Asaph wrote (v. 24a). No action that we take on earth is meaningless. Even the smallest task can have eternal significance. Our God desires to serve as our career counselor, guiding us day in and day out with precepts that make our jobs meaningful and our lives abundant. As Jesus said, "I have come that they may have life, and have it to the full" (John 10:10).

God leads us into a glorious afterlife. With God we have a companion who not only leads us while we are here—he also delivers us safely to our next location! "Afterward you will take me into glory" (Psalm 73:24b). "And if I go and prepare a place for you," Jesus promised, "I will come back and take you to be with me that you also may be where I am" (John 14:3). How can a child feel lonely when he grasps the Father's hand!

BIBLE**TRUTH** 3

God will give us what no one else has.
PSALM 73:25, 26

■ **Why do you think people fear death?**

INSIDE STORY: Facing our own mortality without companionship is frightening. Dying alone is almost too dreadful to contemplate. Asaph affirmed, "My flesh and my heart may fail, but God is the strength of my heart and my portion forever" (v. 26). All of us will grow weaker, and we will die. Yet we have a source of true security. This earth and the entire spiritual realm have nothing greater than what we hold as a child of God (v. 25). We will not die alone.

CHALLENGE

Play a pop song in which a singer complains of loneliness. Ask your group to try to answer that complaint using the principles of this study.

CHRISTIAN FRIENDS ARE INVALUABLE!

CONFIDENTIAL SOURCE:
PHILEMON 8-16;
HEBREWS 10:24

What makes a real friend?

Limits of Loyalty

Homemaker extraordinaire Martha Stewart seems to have an unlimited supply of recipes and time to prepare the delicacies. A few years ago, however, she seemed to have a shortage of friends to whom to serve them.

For several months, Stewart was been questioned about her involvement in an insider-trading scheme involving a drug company called ImClone Systems. "Insider trading" is the illegal practice of buying or selling stock in a company after you have been given important information about that company that's not yet available to the general public.

Martha Stewart owned about 4,000 shares of ImClone, valued at hundreds of thousands of dollars. All at once, Stewart sold that stock. Investigators alleged that she sold it because she received inside information that the Food and Drug Administration (FDA) would not approve ImClone's cancer-fighting drug Erbitux. After that information was made public, ImClone's stock price plummeted. Had Stewart not sold early, she would have lost a lot of money.

Last week, real estate broker and friend of Stewart, Mariana Pasternak, agreed to cooperate with federal investigators in order to receive a reduced sentence. Pasternak, whose husband also owned and sold a large amount of ImClone stock, was traveling with Stewart when the celebrity allegedly sold her stock. Pasternak testified that she and Stewart received inside information from someone, possibly ImClone's founder and chief executive Samuel Waksal, before selling the stock.

Waksal made a different decision than did Pasternak. He pleaded innocent to the charges against him and refused to make a deal with prosecutors. The deal would have required him to reveal, in exchange for a reduced sentence, whether he provided insider trading tips to family and friends, including Martha Stewart.

Stewart was tried and found guilty of conspiracy, obstruction of an agency proceeding, and making false statements to federal investigators and sentenced to serve a five-month term in a federal correctional facility and a two-year period of supervised release (to include five months of home confinement).

QUESTIONS TO CONSIDER:

■ Contrast Pasternak's and Waksal's decisions to deal with investigators. Whom do you think Martha Stewart would count as a better friend? Do you think she would be right? Explain.

■ Agree or disagree: "A friend defends you, even when you are wrong." What characteristics do *you* believe mark a true friend?

■ We have taken a look at what we think makes a good friend. In Philemon 8-16 we find three characteristics demonstrated by Paul and some of his closest Christian friends.

BIBLE TRUTHS

BIBLE**TRUTH** 1

Christian friendship allows us to make bold demands out of mutual love.
PHILEMON 8, 9; HEBREWS 10:24

■ **What types of things can you say to a good friend but not to anyone else? What requests can you make only to a true friend?**

INSIDE STORY: Paul wrote to a friend and believer (Philemon) on behalf of another friend and believer (Onesimus). Onesimus was Philemon's slave who escaped and was later captured in Rome. While imprisoned together, Paul and Onesimus discovered that they had a mutual acquaintance, but more importantly, Onesimus became a Christian. In the Roman Empire at that time, what Onesimus had done could have been punished by death. Slavery was an accepted part of the social order of the Roman Empire. While sowing seeds of love, respect, and brotherhood that would eventually undermine the practice of slavery, the early Christians did not directly confront it (1 Corinthians 7:21-24; Ephesians 6:5-9; Colossians 3:22-24; 1 Peter 2:18-21). Suggesting that Onesimus be reinstated without further punishment was a radical suggestion. Instead of making demands, Paul encouraged Philemon to do right on the basis of love (Philemon 8, 9; Hebrews 10:24).

BIBLE**TRUTH** 2

Christian friendship binds unlikely people together. PHILEMON 10, 11

■ **They say, "Birds of a feather flock together." Do you think this is always true of friendships? Explain.**

INSIDE STORY: While the world divides people into groups, Christ breaks those barriers (Ephesians 2:14). Class distinctions are meaningless in the church, because all are saved by grace. An educated Jew like Paul and a Gentile slave would have had little in common. Yet because of the work of Christ, Paul considered his relationship with the former slave as one of a father and son (v. 10). Paul played on Onesimus's name (meaning *useful*) when he said,

"[Onesimus] was useless to you, but now he has become useful both to you and to me" (Philemon 11).

Another example is the church of Antioch. This church was one of the first to contain Jews and Gentiles (Acts 11:19-21). Among the elders of the church were Simon called Niger (meaning "the black one") and Manaen who grew up in the household of Herod (Acts 13:1). The Antioch church brought together Jews and Gentiles, black and white, and even slave and royalty! The church of Jesus brings people together.

BIBLE**TRUTH** 3

Christian friendship supercedes all other human relationships. PHILEMON 15, 16

■ **How are family relationships even deeper than friendships? Why do you think the church is called the family of God?**

INSIDE STORY: Imagine the tension that should have existed between Philemon and Onesimus. A runaway slave had returned. Wouldn't it just make good business sense for Philemon to enforce a "zero tolerance" policy upon any future negative behaviors from Onesimus? It would just make sense that Philemon rule his slave with an iron hand. Paul asked Philemon to do more than accept his slave back without further repercussions. He asked Philemon to treat Onesimus "no longer as a slave, but better than a slave, as a dear brother" (v. 16). Christian friendship was more important than any business relationship they shared.

The same grace had been applied to Paul. At the time of this writing, Paul was a jailbird! But that did not change Paul's status with either of these men or with anyone else in the church of Colosse. Although he was a prisoner of Rome, the only relationship that mattered was that all of them were prisoners of Christ (v. 9b).

CHALLENGE

Ask your students: What kind of friend are you? Pick three traits that you think describe yourself and keep them in mind. Pick three that you think describe the person on your right and three that you think describe the person on your left.

THE **BIG** TRUTH

GOD CAN BLESS US THROUGH NEW AND UNEXPECTED FRIENDSHIPS.

CONFIDENTIAL SOURCE:
ACTS 9:26-28;
ROMANS 15:5-7

What about cliques?

Game to Take on the World

For more than one hundred years, the professional baseball season in the United States has ended with the World Series. One of two major league teams from the United States or Canada is crowned World Champion. But since baseball has been played all over the world for decades, many players and teams have felt left out. Why should only North American baseball teams compete for this honor? Is it really a "world" series if teams from all over the world are not invited to this exclusive playoff?

Now this issue has been addressed. Professional baseball no longer belongs only to the nation that pioneered it, thanks to the World Baseball Classic.

Major League Baseball (MLB) and its players association conducted the first World Baseball Classic in 2006 with professional leagues and players associations from six of the seven continents of the world. (Sorry, but it seems that there is no professional baseball in Antarctica!) The goal of the tournament was to increase worldwide exposure of the game of baseball and introduce new fans and players to the game.

The 2009 World Baseball Classic began in March with first round play held at sites in Japan, Mexico, Puerto Rico, and Canada. The next rounds were held in the U.S. In all, thirty-nine games were played. Teams from Australia, Canada, China, Chinese Taipei, Cuba, Dominican Republic, Italy, Netherlands, Japan, Korea, Mexico, Panama, Puerto Rico, South Africa, United States, and Venezuela participated in this tournament.

The World Baseball Classic demonstrated that although the rules of the game are the same throughout the world, each nation brings some unique elements to the game. The Cubans, for instance, played with exaggerated, macho displays of emotion, while the Japanese have added style to the tournament with their dyed hair, funky necklaces, garish sunglasses, and four-color practice bats.

Players and fans alike have seen the benefits of international baseball. Chipper Jones of the Atlanta Braves and a member of the U.S. team in 2006 called the WBC "the best baseball experience of my life—bar none." "I feel so happy," said Ramiro Navarro, a security guard from Cuba. "This is a big step forward for Cuban baseball." "I believe it will lift baseball not only in Puerto Rico, but also in other places of the world," predicted San Juan businessman, Carlos Sanchez.

QUESTIONS TO CONSIDER:

■ Did you watch any of the World Baseball Classic? Were you pleased with the outcome? Why or why not? Do you feel that other countries have been excluded unfairly in the past when a "world champion" baseball team was announced? Explain.

■ Tell about a time when you purposely excluded someone from your group of friends. Tell about a time when you were left out of an "in group."

■ The Bible tells us about how Paul was once excluded from an important circle of friends—the apostles! Let's learn what that story can teach us about expanding our own friendships.

INSTANT**STUDY 13** ■ BIBLE**TRUTHS**

31

BIBLE TRUTHS

BIBLE**TRUTH** 1

Take the risk of reaching out to others.
ROMANS 15:5, 7; ACTS 9:26

■ **What are some fears people have that keep them from getting close to others? How rational are these fears? Explain.**

INSIDE STORY: Saul of Tarsus had become infamous in the early church by attempting to destroy it (Acts 9:2). Nevertheless, as he traveled to Damascus, the zealous persecutor of Christians became a zealous preacher of Christ (vv. 3-22). After leaving Damascus, Saul spent three years in Arabia deepening his faith (Galatians 1:11-18). He returned to Damascus and then to Jerusalem. When he tried to join with the church there, he was met with resistance. Even after three years of absence, the presence of Saul still struck fear in the hearts of believers.

Perhaps Paul thought of his experience when he told Christians in Rome, "Accept one another" (Romans 15:7). Paul realized that accepting others required "endurance and encouragement" (v. 5). God's power will not allow his church to be destroyed and will impart the hearts of his people with the courage to accept others.

BIBLE**TRUTH** 2

Confess that you are no more worthy of love than anyone else. ROMANS 15:5-7; ACTS 9:27

■ **List some exclusive clubs. How would you describe the people in them? Do you think such clubs are a good idea? Explain.**

INSIDE STORY: Into Paul's life stepped a man by the name of Barnabas. We first learned of him in Acts 4:36, 37, when he sold land and gave the money to the church. His name was Joseph, and he was a person of such kindness and enthusiasm for others that he was nicknamed Barnabas, a name meaning "Son of Encouragement" (v. 36).

Barnabas set up a meeting between the apostles and Saul and accompanied Saul to that meeting. Barnabas must have built trust between himself and Saul by getting to know him.

Barnabas also must have built a relationship of mutual respect between himself and the apostles. In that meeting he told the apostles how Saul had seen Christ and preached fearlessly in his name. Barnabas acted as Saul's representative in that meeting, testifying for him in his presence. The key is "a spirit of unity," not only between Christians, but also between Christians and those who earnestly seek to know Jesus (Romans 15:5). We are no more worthy of being accepted by Christ than they are (vv. 6, 7).

BIBLE**TRUTH** 3

Praise God for what he does in your life and in the lives of others. ROMANS 15:6, 7; ACTS 9:28

■ **Complete this sentence: "I am so glad I took the time to get to know _____." Why do you feel that way?**

INSIDE STORY: The apostles accepted Saul into their midst, and he continued preaching and debating boldly. So fearless was he that the apostles, apparently concerned for his welfare, sent him back to Tarsus, the city of his birth.

Later when Barnabas needed assistance in ministering to the ethnically diverse and rapidly growing church in Antioch, he went to Tarsus to find Saul (Acts 11:22-26). These two were later sent off together by the prophets and teachers of the Antioch church to begin new churches in Asia Minor (Acts 13:1-3). Paul's acceptance into the church of Jerusalem led to a string of events that culminated in the career of the greatest church planter of the early church. What a difference was made when an outsider was brought inside! God is glorified and praised by such actions (Romans 15:6, 7).

CHALLENGE

Lead a visualized prayer. Have students imagine that Jesus is handing them an invitation to deliver to someone else. That invitation is to join their circle of friends. Whose name is on the invitation? How will they choose to deliver it?

CONFIDENTIAL SOURCE:
1 JOHN 4:7-21

GOD DEFINES "TRUE LOVE" DIFFERENTLY THAN THIS WORLD DOES.

recognize How can I true love?

Cinema Caution

"God sometimes does his work with gentle drizzle, not storms," advised a slave ship captain-turned-clergyman in a remarkable film of a few years ago. And although *Amazing Grace* appeared on only a "drizzle" of less than 800 screens nationwide at first, the movie stormed in to make more money per showing than any other film did the week it premiered.

Amazing Grace told the story of a young British politician named William Wilberforce who lived two centuries ago. Clergyman John Newton (author of the hymn, "Amazing Grace") counseled young Wilberforce to use his position in politics to make slow but significant changes in British society. Wilberforce would later enumerate those changes by saying: "God Almighty has set before me two great objectives—the suppression of the slave trade and the reformation of manners (restoration of Christian morality in society)."

The movie concentrates on the former goal—ending the slave trade in the British Empire. That goal was accomplished on March 25, 1807. But it did not happen overnight. On May 12, 1789, Wilberforce made his first major speech on the subject of abolition in the House of Commons. In his address he reasoned that the trade was morally reprehensible. In January of 1790, Parliament approved his plan to form a committee to investigate the morality of the slave trade. It was only then, after laying two years of groundwork, that Wilberforce introduced the first Parliamentary Bill to abolish the slave trade in 1791. It was overwhelmingly defeated by 163 votes to 88.

But this was not the end of Wilberforce's battle. In fact, it was the beginning of a long campaign, during which Wilberforce introduced a motion in favor of abolition during every session of parliament. Finally, sixteen years later, the bill passed, by a vote of 283 to 16.

So what has become of *Amazing Grace*, the movie that tells the story of this great man? The film drew respectable crowds as more and more theaters decided to show it. Now on DVD, the movie is used in many classrooms to discuss the important work of the great man it features.

QUESTIONS TO CONSIDER:

■ Have you seen the film, *Amazing Grace?* Why or why not? Why do you think that it opened in only about one-fourth the number of theaters that big-name films are shown in when it premiered? What do you think theater owners wanted to know before deciding to show this or any other film?

■ Consider the campaign of Wilberforce to end the slave trade. If you were he, what would you have wanted to know before starting such a campaign? What do you think Wilberforce *did* know for certain that kept his battle going?

■ Tell about a time when you wish you knew what you were getting into before starting a project. Tell what you think this statement means: "Hindsight is always 20/20."

■ Wilberforce was convinced that God was on his side in his battle, even though the odds were against him. We would like to know that we are going to be successful before starting something. When we seek a loving relationship with someone else, we would like assurance that it will turn out well. The Bible gives us wisdom that helps us to have God on our side before we begin to date.

INSTANT **STUDY 14** ■ BIBLE**TRUTHS**

33

BIBLE TRUTHS

BIBLE**TRUTH** 1

Love is demonstrated by the surrender of oneself.
1 JOHN 4:7-10

■ **In the 1960s people spoke of *free love*. In your opinion, can love ever be free? Defend your view.**

INSIDE STORY: To know the truth about love, we have to go to the source. Love comes from God (v. 7); love is what God is all about (v. 8). When God created Adam and Eve, he made them in his own image—with the capacity to love. Love only exists because God exists. Love is part of his nature.

God has demonstrated what it means to love. The ultimate demonstration of love is the giving of God's Son (vv. 9, 10). It is interesting that the first mention of love in Scripture does not occur until Genesis 22. The context of that mention is remarkable. It is the story of the testing of Abraham. His love was tested by his willingness to give up his one and only son (v. 2)! Real love is about giving, not getting.

BIBLE**TRUTH** 2

Love is demonstrated by making the one who is loved feel safe. 1 JOHN 4:13-18

■ **Why is trust an important component of love? What happens to love if trust is not present?**

INSIDE STORY: When someone expresses an interest in buying a piece of property, it is customary that the potential buyer gives the owner of the property a payment known as "earnest money." That payment demonstrates that the one interested in the property will complete the transaction. God has promised to buy (redeem) us. That transaction will not be complete until the end of this age when God's people are taken to live with him forever (Revelation 21:1-4). But in the meantime, we are given God's "earnest money," the Holy Spirit (1 John 4:13; 2 Corinthians 5:5; Ephesians 4:30).

Love is built on trust, not fear. Our love—for God and from God—gives us a sense of confidence, even about the future Judgment Day. We do not fear that God will back out of his promise to redeem us. Perfect love drives out fear (1 John 4:18).

BIBLE**TRUTH** 3

Love is demonstrated when the one who is loved loves others. 1 JOHN 4:11, 12, 19-21

■ **It has been said that love is the only thing that you have more of when you give it away. Do you agree? Explain.**

INSIDE STORY: We don't really have love until we give it away (v. 11). When we love each other, God lives in us and his love is completed in us (v. 12). John does not intend that we love each other to pay God back for loving us. That is impossible. Love is not something we human beings can create on our own. We love because God's love changes our nature so that we are able to love.

Paul had a similar message to Christians in Ephesus, "Be imitators of God, . . . and live a life of love" (Ephesians 5:1, 2). To imitate God in the way we love means that our love will be giving, sharing, trusting (1 John 4:9, 11, 18). If we become genuine children of God, our love will be like his. The perfect example of the Father's love, of course, is Jesus. He loved us and gave himself up for us (Ephesians 5:2, 25).

We love people because they make us think of God. Although we cannot see God, part of his image is reflected in the people we love (1 John 4:20). True love will identify and adore what is like God in the person we love.

CHALLENGE #3 Choose a few secular love songs (make sure they are appropriate) ahead of time, and play clips of these songs for your class. Help students compare and contrast love as described in a song to a biblical definition.

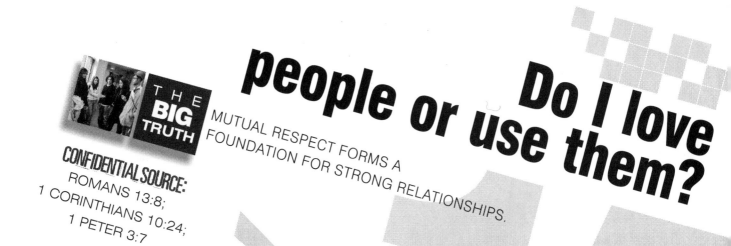

Do I love people or use them?

MUTUAL RESPECT FORMS A FOUNDATION FOR STRONG RELATIONSHIPS.

CONFIDENTIAL SOURCE:
ROMANS 13:8;
1 CORINTHIANS 10:24;
1 PETER 3:7

Paying Respects

During the same week in 2007, tragedy took the lives of several teens. Friends and families gathered to pay their respects.

On Thursday, March 1, eight students of Enterprise (Alabama) High School died as a tornado caused the roof of the building to collapse. Classes were cancelled that week as arrangements to reopen the school were made and funerals were held. Counselor Jim Douhame stressed the importance of parents, students, and school staff taking time to mourn the loss. "I tell them to grieve. Do not stop grieving. If they want to cry, cry. I tell them not to do it alone. If they stop the grieving, it's just going to hurt them in the long run."

During Sunday services at First Baptist Church in the town, the minister thanked Superintendent Jim Reese for his service to the community. The congregation responded with a standing ovation. After church, a line formed of people waiting to hug Reese, shake his hand, or offer words of encouragement. Nancy Jennings, a math teacher at the school, said, "I just want everybody to really keep these families in their prayers because those were precious children that were lost, and we all feel like they were our family."

On Friday, March 2, another tragedy took student lives in a bus accident in Georgia. Four members of the Bluffton (Ohio) University baseball team were killed when the bus driver mistook an exit ramp for a regular lane and drove the bus through a barrier and off of the overpass, onto the highway below. The driver and his wife also died in the crash.

As soon as news of the accident reached the campus, Bluffton University President James M. Harder addressed the media, faculty, staff, and community members. "This is a profoundly tragic and sad day for the Bluffton University campus community," he said. "We are appreciative of the support we have been receiving from individuals and institutions both local and national. Our students and campus community are a close-knit family, and all are deeply impacted by the unfolding events." In a further show of respect to the students and their families, Citizens National Bank in Bluffton has established a fund for them.

QUESTIONS
TO CONSIDER:

■ When someone dies, we often refer to the funeral as the chance for people to "pay their last respects." What does that phrase mean to you? From the incidents described above, list some specific ways people demonstrated respect to those whose lives were taken or drastically changed as a result of tragedy.

■ Respect is not only shown for the dead. There are many ways we show respect to living people each day. Whom do you respect? Why do you count that person worthy of respect? How do you demonstrate such respect? How does the demonstration of respect build relationships you have with people? Give at least one example.

■ While paying last respects is important, respect is even more vital in our relationships with those closest to us. As we continue to talk about dating relationships, we must consider the necessity of respect in those relationships. Let's examine what the Bible says about relationships of respect.

INSTANT **STUDY 15** ■ **BIBLETRUTHS**

35

BIBLE TRUTHS

BIBLE**TRUTH** 1

Respect is a debt we owe others. ROMANS 13:8

■ **Say that you owe a friend a lot of money. In your daily interactions with that friend, how might that debt affect your behavior?**

INSIDE STORY: Most of us think about debt as it pertains to money. We aren't used to thinking of debts when it comes to our relationships. And there is another twist that God adds here; we will never fully pay off the debt of love and respect we owe others (v. 8). Even though we owe it to others, we must remember that we will not automatically receive it. In one of Jesus' parables, a landowner sent his own son to collect from his tenants, thinking they would respect his son simply because of his identity. Instead, he was killed along with the owner's servants (Matthew 21:35-39). Receiving respect is never automatic. Respect, however, can be earned. Scripture teaches that often if we live a life reflecting God's character, especially marked with kindness, then others will have a tendency to respect us (1 Thessalonians 4:11, 12; Proverbs 11:16).

BIBLE**TRUTH** 2

Respect is forgoing our right for another.
1 CORINTHIANS 10:24

■ **Tell about a time that you "stood up for your rights." What were the results?**

INSIDE STORY: There are at least three reasons why giving up our rights out of respect for another can be quite a challenge.

It goes against our nature. Since Adam and Eve, the tendency of human nature is to be selfish. The Bible instructs us to be concerned about the interests of others and to work to actively please our neighbor (Philippians 2:4; Romans 15:2). We must shift from the gear of pleasing oneself to the gear of pleasing others.

Making respect a priority in relationships also *goes against our culture.* Media advertising urges the consumer to make personal pleasure the number one motivation of most every purchasing decision. In contrast, God's Word instructs, "Do nothing out of selfish ambition or vain conceit, but in humility consider others better than yourselves" (Philippians 2:3).

Finally, living out relationships of respect *requires a different role model.* In Philippians 2:5 we are told, "Your attitude should be the same as that of Christ Jesus."

BIBLE**TRUTH** 3

Respect for others pleases God. 1 PETER 3:7

■ **Imagine three close friends who loved one another equally. If you mistreated one friend, how would that affect the other friend?**

INSIDE STORY: God makes it clear that improper treatment in our relationships with others can hinder our communication with him (v. 7). We are bombarded with messages about what to respect and not respect. Animal rights activists tell us that it is imperative we respect animals as if they were people. God, on the other hand, has given us control over the animals and even fashioned garments of skins for Adam and Eve after the fall (Genesis 1:28; 3:21). Some environmental activists tell us to respect the earth because it is the source of our existence. God, on the other hand, wants us to love and respect him as creator and serve as caretakers of the glorious creation he has authored (1:1; 2:15). It is extremely important to recognize the value God places on people and the need to respect them. It gives him great pleasure when our respect follows his wishes rather than those in the world around us.

CHALLENGE Respect literally means to look at again. Have a time of silent meditation in which each student attempts to take another look at someone they have not respected, seeing that person through God's eyes.

Is sexual purity really such a big deal?

So Keep It Clean

A number of news items show the importance of keeping things clean and pure.

Clean water—Eight volunteers from University of Massachusetts Amherst returned from the village of Namawanga in Kenya. The team members belonged to Engineers Without Borders (EWB) and went to the African village to design a plan that would provide clean drinking water to 3,000 people there.

For two weeks the team worked with villagers to measure water quality, plan sites for future wells, and fence off clean water sources to keep livestock out of them. The team returned to Namawanga some months later after raising the $10,000 to $15,000 necessary to drill each well.

Clean city—The city of Natchez applied for a grant through the Mississippi Department of Environmental Quality to clean up an ugly problem. People constantly used areas of the city as places to dump trash illegally.

"It's a major problem. It seems like as soon as they clean a dump up, they go right back and start dumping again," said James "Ricky" Gray, city official. "Human nature is if you have a hole in the ground, that's where you're going to put garbage," added Brett Brinegar, city grants coordinator.

Some plans to stop the problem included monitoring certain areas with cameras and offering rewards through Crime Stoppers to people who share information about illegal dumping.

Clean air—A group of energy businesses in Texas announced that they planned to build two clean coal power demonstration plants in that state. TXU Corporation announced that they started the planning process for two integrated gasification combined cycle (IGCC) demonstration plants.

IGCC technology turns coal into a cleaner-burning gas to reduce pollution. At the time, TXU did not yet have estimates for the cost of building these plants or how much electricity they would generate. Nevertheless, they believed that this new process helps provide for energy needs while keeping the air cleaner than more traditional technology. "We're focused on advancing the new technology and getting a firsthand understanding of the IGCC plants," said TXU spokesman.

QUESTIONS TO CONSIDER:

■ Why is the issue of cleanliness so important in each of the stories above? What are some other areas in which it is important to keep something free of contamination?

■ List some items for sale that talk about the importance of being pure or clean. For example, think of commercials for health and beauty products, food, and cleaning products.

■ We all recognize the importance of pure air and water, uncontaminated food, and a city free from litter. But it goes deeper than that. We as people need to be morally pure, especially in our relationships with one another. Let's look at what the Bible says about relationships of purity in a morally polluted world.

BIBLE TRUTHS

BIBLE**TRUTH** 1

God wants us to attain purity as a mark of his presence in us. 1 THESSALONIANS 4:3, 7, 8

■ **Consider your most prized possession. How important to you is it for it to look clean and well maintained? Why?**

INSIDE STORY: When it comes to the issue of God's will, it's easy to concentrate on those issues that seem more urgent but are really less important. Regarding sexual immorality, God makes his will crystal clear (v. 3). Secondly, God has called his followers to be holy, or set apart, because he is (v. 7; Leviticus 11:44; 1 Peter 1:15, 16). We are not to imitate those around us, but we are to imitate our heavenly Father (Ephesians 5:1-3). Finally, when we reject this call to purity, we are discarding our loving God and his indwelling presence (1 Thessalonians 4:8).

BIBLE**TRUTH** 2

Gaining purity is not a one-time event, but a process. 1 THESSALONIANS 4:1, 2

■ **Think of a new car. What does it take to keep it looking new as long as possible? Why is the owner's self-discipline important?**

INSIDE STORY: The apostle Paul says he is really providing a review for those he has already instructed on how to please God (v. 1). In addition to a review, these verses also provide encouragement to those who are already on the right path (v. 1). No one enjoys being continually corrected, while an occasional pat on the back can go a long way. Successful abstinence education programs today incorporate peer encouragement in the process.

Sometimes to keep growing in an area we have to step it up a notch. The athlete may have to practice a little more and the student may have to study more frequently. That seems to be the message of the words, "Now we ask you and urge you . . . to do this more and more" (v. 1). The emphasis on intensity also provides a good opportunity to urge those who may have gotten off the track to get back on. It's not too late to start over.

BIBLE**TRUTH** 3

Purity keeps us from abusing one another. 1 THESSALONIANS 4:4-6

■ **We may talk about treating someone as a "sex object." What does that mean to you? Why is it wrong?**

INSIDE STORY: The intimacy of sexuality leaves partners vulnerable to be hurt in a relationship. Purity decreases that vulnerability. Self-control is fruit that the Holy Spirit can produce in the life of the believer (Galatians 5:23). A young lady can exercise control by dressing and acting in ways that will draw more attention to her personality than her body. A young man can control himself by deciding to never speak of women in a degrading fashion and to keep his eyes from any and all pornographic material.

In guarding purity it is important to note the contrast that God draws between those who have decided to follow him and those who have not (1 Thessalonians 4:5). God's children are to behave differently. It takes a conscious decision and a well thought out strategy for this difference to be lived out.

Finally, guarding one's purity provides protection from negative *consequences* of hurting others and offending God (v. 6). The potential consequences include those that are emotional, physical, and spiritual in nature. It is clear that God desires sexual purity for his children for their own protection.

CHALLENGE

Sexuality was designed to deepen the intimacy of husband and wife (Genesis 2:24). Sexual immorality, on the other hand, uses a person, dehumanizing and devaluing that person. To illustrate, bring your toothbrush to class. Ask why people choose not to buy used toothbrushes. Pray with the class that they will consciously choose not to diminish the worth of someone else by treating them as something to be used.

Does homosexuality fit into God's plan?

The Healey Method

He was born into a working-class family in the west end of Toronto. He battled a rare form of cancer since birth. He became blind before he could walk or talk. And yet rock and jazz guitarist Jeff Healey has left behind a legacy of determination and creativity.

On March 2, 2008, Healey died of cancer at St. Joseph's Health Centre in Toronto at the age of forty-one. Healey lost his sight when he was one year old due to retinoblastoma, a rare cancer of the eyes. His eyes had to be surgically removed, and he was given artificial replacements. During his last year, the cancer spread to his legs and lungs and claimed his life.

Nevertheless, the life of Jeff Healey will be celebrated as a life of victory, not of disability. The Grammy-nominated guitarist came to stardom as the leader of the rock-oriented Jeff Healey Band. Their 1988 album *See the Light* went platinum and featured the hit single, "Angel Eyes." The band helped inspire the 1989 Patrick Swayze film, *Road House*, in which Healey played a prominent role. Healey also shared stages with rock and blues greats such as George Harrison, B.B. King, and Stevie Ray Vaughan.

Though he was blind, Healey taught himself to play the guitar at the age of three. He was able to do so by creating a unique playing style he designed especially for his needs. "Visually, Jeff was an intriguing player to watch, because he played guitar—by any conventional standard—all wrong, with it flat across his lap," recalls Healey's publicist, Richard Flohil. "But he was remarkable, a virtuoso player." That playing style, combined with his blues-oriented vocals, brought Healey fame and a reputation as a musical prodigy since he was a teen.

Jeff Healey is survived by his wife, Christie, his three-year-old son, and his thirteen-year-old daughter. Because of them, he preferred to stay close to home. "I've traveled widely before—been there and done that," he told friends. During these past years he preferred the life of a disc jockey, playing his favorite jazz music rather than the lengthy, exhausting tours that marked his life in his twenties and early thirties. Healey's final CD, *A Mess of Blues*, was released a month after his death.

QUESTIONS TO CONSIDER:

■ What had you known (if anything) about Jeff Healey before reading this article? What facts about Healey especially impress or surprise you? Explain.

■ Consider the unique guitar-playing method of Jeff Healey. Why might this method be custom-made for someone who was blind? Why might this same method not be suitable for someone who was not blind? Think of some other methods or items that are specifically designed with a certain user in mind (for example, a baseball glove meant for a person who throws with his or her left hand). Why might the same method or item *not* be suitable for some other user?

■ Jeff Healey created a style of playing the guitar that worked very well for him but would be considered clumsy, ineffective, and just plain wrong for someone else. Likewise, God specifically designed the human body to be used in certain ways. But when the purpose of that design is ignored and the body is used in ways not intended by God, problems can occur. Let's see how that fact relates to God's perspective on a controversial issue of our day—homosexuality.

INSTANT**STUDY 17** ■ **BIBLE**TRUTHS

BIBLE TRUTHS

BIBLETRUTH 1

Homosexuality, like all sin, brings judgment.

1 CORINTHIANS 6:9, 10

■ **Why do you think some people have a problem believing homosexuality is wrong?**

INSIDE STORY: A popular view of God teaches that since he loves, he will exact no consequence for any sin. But the Bible also teaches us that God is just (Deuteronomy 32:4) and cannot let rebellion against him go unpunished.

Those who willfully live in sin will not share in the inheritance God plans for his children. "Do you not know that the wicked will not inherit the kingdom of God? Do not be deceived: Neither the sexually immoral nor idolaters nor adulterers nor male prostitutes nor homosexual offenders nor thieves nor the greedy nor drunkards nor slanderers nor swindlers will inherit the kingdom of God" (1 Corinthians 6:9, 10). John echoes these thoughts in his vision of a new Heaven and new earth. "Outside [of the gates of new Jerusalem] are the dogs, those who practice magic arts, the sexually immoral, the murderers, the idolaters and everyone who loves and practices falsehood" (Revelation 22:15).

But many in our society believe that God does accept unrepentant homosexuals. In November of 2003, the Episcopal church consecrated the Reverend Gene Robinson as a bishop of the New Hampshire diocese. Robinson admits to being a practicing homosexual. While many in the church argued that ordaining a gay church leader violated Scripture, others disagreed. The Reverend Douglas Theuner, whom Robinson replaced as bishop, said to Robinson, "You are no more or less a child of God like everyone else. . . . What a joy it is to have you here."

Regardless of what many in society and even in some churches are saying, the Bible teaches that homosexual behavior is sinful. The Bible further teaches that such behavior will be judged. Popular opinion does not alter God's law.

BIBLETRUTH 2

Homosexuality, like all sin, can be conquered by the blood of Christ. 1 CORINTHIANS 6:11

■ **Why do you think some people have a problem believing that God can forgive homosexuality?**

INSIDE STORY: We must not fail to point out that homosexuality is a sin and an abomination to God. We also must not fail to proclaim the power of salvation in Jesus Christ to all who come to him—to the homosexual as well as to the heterosexual. Jesus loves everyone, including the homosexual offender. He loves us too much to leave us the way we are. He wants to change us and to help us live a life of holiness.

After speaking of the judgment of God leveled at unrepentant sinners, Paul concluded by saying, "And that is what some of you were. But you were washed, you were sanctified, you were justified in the name of the Lord Jesus Christ and by the Spirit of our God" (v. 11).

People may get caught up in sin, including homosexuality. But there is no sin that Jesus didn't die for, there is no sin he cannot forgive, and there is no sinner we should not love.

Westboro Baptist Church of Topeka, Kansas, has chosen to be known for its outspoken hatred of homosexuals. The main Web page for the church is called godhatesfags.com. In strong opposition to this view, Paul taught that God loves sinners and seeks to change them.

Homosexuality violates the purposes for which God designed men and women and sex and marriage. Though our society teaches many untrue things about homosexuality, the Bible is clear about its *cause*, *consequence*, and *cure*.

CHALLENGE

Read Ephesians 4:15, stressing the words *truth* and *love*. Discuss how both of those words deal with the church and homosexuality. Have students draw a line graph with one of those two words at either end. Ask students to plot their own attitudes about homosexuality on that graph. What do they need to do to move more toward the center where biblical truth and unconditional love are in perfect balance?

INSTANT **STUDY** 17 . . . CONTINUED

40

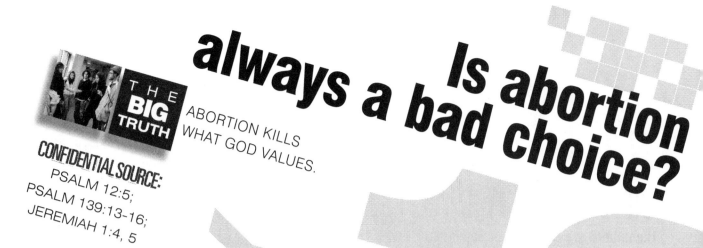

always a bad choice? Is abortion

THE BIG TRUTH

ABORTION KILLS
WHAT GOD VALUES.

CONFIDENTIAL SOURCE:
PSALM 12:5;
PSALM 139:13-16;
JEREMIAH 1:4, 5

Making It Pig

They will never win a Grammy. But when thirty British farmers teamed together to record a song at a British studio a few years ago, they were not thinking of winning an award. Instead, they were trying to express their feelings about their true love—raising hogs.

Their song was a parody of the 1968 Tammy Wynette country music classic, "Stand By Your Man." The recording of "Stand By Your Ham," is the work of Britain's National Pig Association (NPA).

What "Stand By Your Ham" lacked in musicianship, it more than made up with teamwork and passion for their porkers. The tune told of the financial crisis being faced by those who raise hogs in Britain. Steep increases in feed prices and competition from pig farmers in other European countries caused the pig industry in that country to lose an estimated six pounds (about $12 in U.S. currency) every second.

While they were concerned about their own finances, farmers argued that the issue was also the humane treatment of hogs. British animal welfare standards are among the highest in the world. It has been said that 70 percent of the pork imported from other countries would be illegal to produce in England. In the song the farmers sang, "'Cause we take good care of our pigs. We are so proud of them. To us they're more than pork and ham."

A NPA survey showed that 95 percent of pig farmers considered stopping production if the price they receive did not improve. This could lead to a shortage of pig meat in the long term and potentially steep rises in the retail price of pork, sausages, bacon, and ham.

"It's a lighthearted way of drawing attention to a very serious issue," asserted Yorkshire pig farmer Richard Longthorp. Barney Kay, NPA general manager and the man behind "Stand By Your Ham," said: "It is a slightly tongue in cheek way of raising awareness of a serious issue. Put simply, farmers need to receive more for their pigs or many face the prospect of going out of business. All they are asking for is a fair price."

QUESTIONS
TO CONSIDER:

■ What is your reaction to the above article? Did it make you laugh? Did it make you think? Why? Why do you think it is important to British pig farmers that hogs are treated humanely? How much truth do you think is in the lyric, "'Cause we take good care of our pigs. We are so proud of them"?

■ The NPA farmers are proud of their work and of the pigs they raise. Tell about a time when you have been proud of something you have created or accomplished. How would it make you feel if others treated it as unimportant?

■ Pig farmers in Britain care that the pigs that are raised to be slaughtered for ham and bacon be treated humanely while they are alive. Most people would agree that animal life should not be treated cruelly. Ironically, not all people feel the same way about much more important lives—the lives of unborn children. Let's look at why God considers unborn human life so valuable.

BIBLE TRUTHS

BIBLE**TRUTH** 1

The unborn are creations of God. PSALM 139:13–15

■ **How might people feel if great works of art were destroyed? Compare and contrast unborn children to artistic masterpieces.**

INSIDE STORY: David knew that God is the creator of the "inmost being" of every unborn baby, a special creation that he has "knit . . . together" (v. 13). Notice God's loving attention to detail when creating a work of living art. God's works are masterpieces, "fearfully and wonderfully made" (v. 14).

Imagine how much more David would have marveled if he knew what we know today. In the human body there are over 100 trillion cells, and every cell has its strip of DNA with a precise sequence of over three billion bits of information. Long before birth this miracle of God's design is evident. Within six weeks of conception, for instance, the tiny brain is visible and electrically active. Every minute until birth, another 100,000 nerve cells are produced and "wired" into place, allowing the baby in the womb to react to light, noise, music, or pain.

BIBLE**TRUTH** 2

God has plans for the unborn.

PSALM 139:16; JEREMIAH 1:4, 5

■ **Have you ever seen the classic film *It's a Wonderful Life*? What does it say about the value of a single life?**

INSIDE STORY: David declared, "All the days ordained for me were written in your book before one of them came to be" (Psalm 139:16). Without David, how would Israel have withstood Goliath? Who would have written the songs of worship that still inspire believers today? What would have happened to the line of kings that came after him, including Jesus, the King of kings? What would have happened if David had never been born? Abortion not only destroys God's workmanship, it also derails God's plans for the future.

God echoed David's words when speaking to the prophet Jeremiah. "Before I formed you in the womb I knew you" (Jeremiah 1:5). Unlike David, Jeremiah's legacy was not so

dramatic. Jeremiah has been described as the only preacher in the Bible who failed to win a convert. He did not father a line of kings or shape the policies of a nation. But God also had plans for Jeremiah. From the greatest of kings to the most reviled of prophets to people like us today, God creates with a mission in mind. Abortion thwarts that mission.

BIBLE**TRUTH** 3

God wants the helpless to be protected.

PSALM 12:5

■ **List some laws that protect the weakest members of society. Why do we have such laws?**

INSIDE STORY: The Scripture clearly teaches that the weakest members of society have a special place in God's heart (v. 5). We must be careful if we pick on the helpless. In doing so, we make God angry. God wants justice for those who are unable to care for themselves (9:9; 10:17, 18). The law of Moses commanded that the people of Israel were not to mistreat foreigners who lived among them (Exodus 22:21; Leviticus 19:33, 34). They were not to take advantage of widows and orphans and not to cheat those who needed to borrow money (Exodus 22:22-27). The law further forbade the abuse of people who suffered from physical disabilities such as being blind or deaf (Leviticus 19:14). What is God's attitude toward the weakest members of society? God will not stand idly by while people abuse the weak.

CHALLENGE

Secure permission ahead of time and take your students to visit your church nursery. Spend a few minutes there, allowing the students, if possible, to interact with the infants and toddlers. Pray together for the future of these children as well as for children yet to be born.

How can I improve my relationships with others?

THE BIG TRUTH

HEALTHY RELATIONSHIPS JUST DON'T "HAPPEN;" THEY ARE DEVELOPED.

CONFIDENTIAL SOURCE:
TITUS 2:11, 12;
1 PETER 3:3, 4; JOB 31:1;
JAMES 3:17

It Seemed Like a Good Idea . . .

It may have seemed like a good idea at the time, but perhaps the artist should have done a little more preparation. A work of Spanish-born artist, Santiago Sierra, was on display for only one day.

A day after it premiered, the city of Pulheim-Stommeln (Germany) and the Jewish community asked Sierra to cancel his showing of a "trangressive art" exhibit entitled *245 Kubikmeter.* Transgressive art involves displays that break cultural taboos and unspoken rules of propriety. Sierra's work did exactly that. His exhibit involved pumping carbon monoxide fumes from six running cars into an abandoned Jewish synagogue and inviting people to enter that toxic environment.

During World War II, at least 750,000 Jews were asphyxiated with motor exhaust fumes in death camps at nearby Chelmno and Belzec. Sierra claimed that he "did not and does not wish to insult or hurt anyone" but only wanted to show how real and horrible the gas chambers were. He was trying to do that by allowing people to experience a working gas chamber firsthand.

Visitors to *245 Kubikmeter* (named because the volume of the synagogue is 245 cubic meters) had to sign a disclaimer, put on a gas mask, and enter the makeshift gas chamber with a firefighter especially hired for the exhibit. The local fire department refused to cooperate with the exhibit.

A local survey discovered that there was some disagreement as to whether turning a synagogue into a gas chamber was an appropriate way to remember victims of Nazi genocide. The survey showed that 27 percent of people found the project provocative and "acceptable." On the other hand, 38 percent considered the exhibit "tasteless and reprehensible."

Stephan J. Kramer, the head of the Jewish central advisory council in Germany, complained that the work "goes way beyond the limits of what's acceptable" and is "insulting to the victims" of the Holocaust. "If this is the new form of memory," said Kramer, "then should we reopen Auschwitz and hand out gas masks to the visitors so that they can get the real experience?"

Although the town claims that the exhibit was closed only to allow time to debate, it is unlikely that it will ever reopen.

QUESTIONS
TO CONSIDER:

■ Why do you think *245 Kubikmeter* met such resistance? What is your opinion of the exhibit? What are some ways that Sierra could have been better prepared for the reaction to his project?

■ What are some common things in life for which we have to prepare? How does preparation save us a lot of hurt and embarrassment? Tell about a time when you experienced unnecessary hurt or embarrassment because you did not prepare well.

■ Opening a controversial art exhibit certainly requires preparation. But today we'll take a look at an even more important endeavor that requires us to be prepared—establishing dating relationships. Let's see what God has to say about equipping ourselves to have healthy relationships.

BIBLE TRUTHS

BIBLE**TRUTH** 1

We prepare for relationships by gaining self-control. TITUS 2:11, 12

■ **Sometimes we admire the life of a rebel who does whatever he wants. But what are the drawbacks in a relationship with him?**

INSIDE STORY: Paul left Titus on the island of Crete to lead the church there. Although the citizens of Crete had the reputation of being "liars, evil brutes, lazy gluttons" (1:12), the Christians were to rise above their culture. Paul told Titus to instruct them to be self-controlled and pure (2:4-6). Paul said the grace of God has appeared, bringing salvation (or "wholeness") to mankind (v. 11). For the believers in Crete, this meant that although they lived in a broken and corrupt society, they were being made whole and restored to the life God intended. God's grace taught them to say "No" to worldly passions and to live self-controlled and godly lives.

BIBLE**TRUTH** 2

We prepare for relationships by dressing up our inner beauty. 1 PETER 3:3, 4

■ **The old saying states, "Beauty is only skin deep." What does that mean to you?**

INSIDE STORY: Another part of getting ready to meet new people is trying to achieve just the right "look." The hair, the clothes, the jewelry, the makeup—everything has to be exactly right. The apostle Peter, however, gave some sound advice for women who were trying to impress their husbands. Their beauty should not come from the outside. It was not their hairdo or their gold jewelry or their fine clothes that made them beautiful (v. 3). Their real beauty came from the inner self, where their gentle and quiet spirit had the approval of God (v. 4).

BIBLE**TRUTH** 3

We prepare for relationships by understanding our core values. JOB 31:1

■ **List some unbreakable rules you have for your life. How well could you get along with someone with different rules? Explain.**

INSIDE STORY: Jesus warned that the heart is the source of evil thoughts, adultery, and sexual immorality (Matthew 15:19). Getting the heart right, therefore, is an important part of avoiding wrong behavior.

Long ago, this is what Job had in mind when he said, "I have made a covenant with my eyes not to look lustfully at a girl" (Job 31:1). As Job held fast to his integrity and innocence to the men who were accusing him, it was important that he could affirm that he had lived by this commitment. Job knew that his heart was right.

BIBLE**TRUTH** 4

We prepare for relationships by seeking to have a godly mind. JAMES 3:17

■ **When have you acted before thinking through a situation? What were some results of your actions?**

INSIDE STORY: The mind must not be ignored when improving relationships. Genuine wisdom is pure (v. 17). Even if an idea is something "everybody knows" about relationships, if it is not pure, it is not wise. Furthermore, for a relationship to be strong it must center on peace not conflict, mercy not judgment, and personal growth not apathy (v. 17). We need to think about what relationships should be and not be driven by emotion.

CHALLENGE Brainstorm a list of relationship problems and prescribe one or more of the biblical principles studied to help remedy each problem.

What about hypocrites?

Substitute Student

Schools of all sorts are used to having substitute teachers. But Stanford University had to deal with something much more unusual—a substitute *student*!

University officials discovered that eighteen-year-old Azia Kim from Fullerton, California, spent the entire school year living as a Stanford student. For eight months, Miss Kim posed as a biology major, buying textbooks, sneaking into meals, and even moving in with unsuspecting roommates.

The preceding September, Kim told two sophomores that she did not like the dorm roommate she was assigned. The trusting students allowed her to stay with them. In April, Stanford student Amy Zhou needed a roommate, and Kim was referred to her. She was welcomed into the smaller dorm specifically for Asian students, where the sign on the resident advisor's door read, "My house is your house." Since Miss Kim was never officially a student, she was never issued a key to the room. She kept a window of the first-floor room open by which she entered.

While at one time the case of the substitute student might have been seen as an elaborate prank, concern for campus security in light of the tragic Virginia Tech massacre caused a much more serious reaction. "Personally, I don't feel safe now that Stanford allowed this to happen and that they're not doing anything to ensure the safety of their students," responded Amy Zhou after the ruse was discovered.

"We consider these allegations, if confirmed, to be a serious breach of security within the residence halls," Greg Boardman, Stanford's vice provost for student affairs, promised. "We are conducting a full investigation into what occurred and how security can be improved." Results of the university's investigation will be submitted to the district attorney, who will decide whether or not to prosecute Kim.

Criminal charges aside, Miss Kim's deception could have been costly for her. Stanford charges a $175 per day fee for visitors to stay on campus. Even though Kim did all the work of a student but earned no college credits, she could have been charged $44,000 for her stay. That is the same bill she would have received if she were an *actual*, rather than a *virtual*, student.

QUESTIONS
TO CONSIDER:

■ Describe your reaction to the unusual tale of Miss Azia Kim. Would your reaction be any different if you had come to trust her as a fellow student on the Stanford campus? Why or why not?

■ The article tells us that Kim may have to pay the same fee as she would have if she were a real student. Try to list some other disadvantages of being a substitute student that Kim faced. Why would someone choose to be a substitute rather than the real thing? Have you ever pretended to be someone you were not? Tell about that time.

■ Substitutes are often inadequate replacements for the real thing. Such was certainly the case with Azia Kim. She lost more than she gained in pretending to be a university student. In Jesus' day there were also "substitute students." These men, the scribes and Pharisees, pretended to study God's Word seriously but were frauds at heart. Let's discover some problems associated with being a substitute student of God.

BIBLE TRUTHS

BIBLE**TRUTH** 1

Hypocrites know God's Word but do not apply it to themselves. MATTHEW 23:2-4

■ **People used to say, "Do as I say, not as I do." What is wrong with that type of thinking?**

INSIDE STORY: The first sad truth about hypocrites is that they know better. Jesus told his followers to obey what the law-teachers and Pharisees said, because what they taught was true. The problem was that they did not practice what they preached (v. 3). They talked the talk—correctly!—but they did not walk the walk. They loved to load people up with God's commands, but they would not lift a finger to carry that load themselves (v. 4). Contrast this to the call to Christian leaders to live consistent lives as examples to others (Titus 2:7; 1 Peter 5:3).

BIBLE**TRUTH** 2

Hypocrites want to draw attention to their positions. MATTHEW 23:5-7, 12

■ **How does it make you feel to be around people who try to draw attention to themselves? Explain your feelings.**

INSIDE STORY: The second sad truth about hypocrites is that everything they do is done for people to see (v. 5). The hypocritical Pharisees strapped leather boxes containing Scripture on their arms and foreheads (Deuteronomy 6:6-8). They put extra-long tassels on their outer garments (Numbers 15:37-41). They loved public honors and fancy titles (Matthew 23:6, 7). Jesus warned that only those who sincerely humble themselves will be exalted (v. 12). Like Jesus, they are willing to give up power to quietly serve (Philippians 2:5-7).

BIBLE**TRUTH** 3

Hypocrites care more about making people follow rules than leading them to know God. MATTHEW 23:13, 15, 23, 25, 27

■ **How have you seen people use religion to try to control people?**

INSIDE STORY: Thirdly, hypocrites *use* people rather than *serve* people. They try to make converts, but men who follow their examples become even worse (v. 15). Contrast this with Paul who was able to point to those whom he led to the Lord as "letters of recommendation" and new creatures (2 Corinthians 3:1-3; 5:17).

Hypocrites play games with God's Word. Pharisees counted out a tenth of the spices they grew and gave God his share (Matthew 23:23). They carefully gave their cups and dishes the proper ceremonial washing (v. 25). But they ignored what the law was really all about—things like justice, mercy, and faithfulness. Jesus said they were like whitewashed tombs: pretty on the outside, but defiled on the inside (v. 27).

BIBLE**TRUTH** 4

Hypocrites are harmful to God's kingdom. MATTHEW 23:29-31, 34-38

■ **What is a *martyr*? Can you name some?**

INSIDE STORY: Finally, hypocrites do great damage to God's kingdom. Jesus accused the law-teachers and Pharisees of sharing in their forefathers' persecution of the spokesmen of God (vv. 29-31). In fact, their persecution of prophets was continuing (vv. 34-37). Hypocrites always opposed a real spokesman for God.

Because Jerusalem allowed hypocritical leaders to damage God's kingdom, the city would suffer bloodshed and desolation (vv. 35, 38). In the end, hypocrites will get what they deserve. In contrast, helpful Christian leaders will be remembered and rewarded (1 Timothy 5:17; Hebrews 13:7).

CHALLENGE

Pharisees wore small boxes containing Scripture verses on their foreheads as a way of displaying how religious they were. Challenge students to internalize a part of this Bible text with memorization this week.

Does the Bible talk about racial prejudice?

Public Policy and Pants

The state of Florida was angry at the fashion choices of some of the students in its public schools. The Florida Senate then took action to make a particular wardrobe fad illegal.

On Thursday, March 13, 2008, the Florida Senate passed a bill to authorize suspensions for students who wear saggy pants. The bill's sponsor was Democrat Senator Gary Siplin from Orlando. Siplin and other supporters of the bill said that such a bill is necessary to force schools to properly enforce dress codes. They further argued that parents are often not aware that their children leave home dressed inappropriately. Critics of the law said that the measure was unnecessary. They argued that student appearance and dress codes should be the responsibility of schools and parents, not the state legislature. Nevertheless, the bill became law. A circuit court overturned the law six months later, however.

The hip-hop music world is credited with popularizing the fad of wearing pants that droop low enough to expose flesh or underwear. Supposedly the look comes from inmates in prisons where wearing belts have been banned. "All we're trying to do now is trying to inform folks that we have a fad now that does not have a very good origination," Siplin said. "We're trying to make an example in school," he added, saying it would help students get jobs and a degree.

Similar laws have been considered elsewhere. The Florida city of Riviera Beach passed its own saggy pants ordinance. The first offense carries a $150 fine or community service. A second infraction carries a $300 fine or more community service. Repeat offenders may receive a maximum penalty of sixty days in jail.

In September 2007, the city of Mansfield, Louisiana, passed a law calling for a $150 fine or fifteen days in jail for anyone whose baggy pants exposes his or her underwear. Since November in that same year, the penalty has been $100 in Pine Lawn, Missouri. Cities in Delaware, New Jersey, and Georgia have similar ordinances. A few years ago the state of Virginia also debated a droopy-pants law. The Virginia law would have imposed a $50 fine on people who wore their pants so low that their underwear was visible in "a lewd or indecent manner." The bill was later defeated and has never become law.

QUESTIONS TO CONSIDER:

■ What do think of the fad of wearing droopy pants? Why do you think so many citizens and lawmakers across the country have responded to it? Do you think these laws are fair, or do you believe they treat certain people unjustly? Defend your answer.

■ Some believe such laws discriminate against certain people. Others argue that the target of the law is behavior, not the people themselves. What do you think? Regardless of your stand on baggy pants, think of a situation in which people were really discriminated against because they were different.

■ It is interesting that many people around the country are angered by the saggy pants fad. Laws are sometimes used to protect people from behavior they believe is wrong. On the other hand, sometimes people make rules and even laws that discriminate against people that are different from them. Prejudice is nothing new. Let's look at an instance of prejudice in the Bible and how God reacted to it.

BIBLE TRUTHS

BIBLE **TRUTH** 1

Prejudice is a symptom of a power struggle.
NUMBERS 12:1, 2

■ **What do you think the real reason behind racial prejudice is? How does racism benefit one group over another?**

INSIDE STORY: Moses had led God's people out of bondage in Egypt, and he was leading them from Mt. Sinai to the promised land. But in the midst of his heroic leadership, Moses began to attract criticism from his own sister and brother. Their complaint was that he had married a Cushite woman (v. 1). There is no indication in the text that there was anything morally or spiritually wrong with the woman—it was just that she was a Cushite, not a Jew. (The Cushites were descendants of Ham, who lived in the southern Nile valley in Africa.)

But we see that this issue was an argument raised to hide the arguer's true intent. Miriam and Aaron made the unsubstantiated charge that Moses' marriage to the Cushite woman had diminished his ability to lead God's people. Yet their true aim was to lower Moses' standing so they could elevate their own. "Hasn't [the Lord] also spoken through us?" they asked, intending to take over the role of leadership (v. 2). After all, hadn't Miriam led all the women in praise, and wasn't Aaron chosen by God to be high priest (Exodus 15:20, 21; 28:1)? By putting Moses down, they hoped to gain recognition for themselves.

BIBLE **TRUTH** 2

Prejudice causes us to overlook remarkable people. NUMBERS 12:3-15

■ **Have you ever heard of Negro League Baseball of the early twentieth century? How did racism weaken the game of baseball?**

INSIDE STORY: Since Moses was a very humble man, he said nothing in his own defense, but God at once called Moses, Aaron, and Miriam to the Tabernacle (vv. 3, 4). The Lord came down in a pillar of cloud and commanded, "Listen to my words" (v. 6). God explained that Moses was more than a prophet. To him God spoke clearly, not just in riddles (v. 8). Because Moses was faithful in all God's house, Miriam and Aaron should have been afraid to speak out against him (v. 7). Then, to show that Moses was right and they were wrong, Miriam was struck with leprosy (vv. 10, 12). Aaron cried out in dismay, "Please . . . do not hold against us the sin we have so foolishly committed" (v. 11). In response to their repentance and the prayer of Moses, God reduced her penalty to seven days of exile outside the camp (vv. 13-15).

BIBLE **TRUTH** 3

Prejudice puts us in direct opposition to God.
REVELATION 7:9

■ **How do we know that God hates racism?**

INSIDE STORY: The Great Commission commands us to "make disciples of all nations" (Matthew 28:19). As he worked to fulfill that commission, Paul said of the church, "Here there is no Greek or Jew, circumcised or uncircumcised, barbarian, Scythian, slave or free, but Christ is all, and is in all" (Colossians 3:11). Likewise Peter affirmed, "God does not show favoritism but accepts men from every nation who fear him and do what is right" (Acts 10:34, 35). God's plan for humankind will be complete when all of his people finally gather before his throne in Heaven. There will be "a great multitude that no one could count, from every nation, tribe, people and language" (Revelation 7:9). There will be no room for prejudice in Heaven. Neither is there room for it among God's people now.

CHALLENGE

Sing the old children's song, "Jesus Loves the Little Children," pointing out deep truth in the simple song.

INSTANT **STUDY** 21 . . . CONTINUED

48

Does my reputation matter?

MANY THINGS CAN ATTACK OUR INTEGRITY—
WE MUST GUARD OUR GODLY REPUTATIONS.

Juiced

Two identical containers sat side by side in a cooler at an Applebee's restaurant in California. But very different liquids were inside each one. That difference could end up costing the restaurant dearly.

Two-year-old Julian Mayorga started making funny faces and pushing his spill-proof cup away from him while he and his mother were eating at the local restaurant. Confused, the child's mother opened the cup that she believed contained apple juice. In the cup she found an alcoholic beverage rather than fruit juice.

As a result of ingesting alcohol, Julian became drowsy and began vomiting a few hours later. He was rushed to the hospital for treatment. "I wasn't going to make a big deal about it," said Julian's mother, Kim Mayorga. "But then he got sick."

Agents from the California Department of Alcoholic Beverage Control (ABC) investigated the incident. ABC considered as part of their evaluation whether there was intent. Possible penalties for such an offense range from a warning letter to the repeal of the restaurant's liquor license.

A similar incident occurred in July 2005 at an Applebee's in New York. There a five-year-old boy was served alcohol instead of the apple juice that was ordered in a similar, no-spill cup. The mother in that case sued the restaurant.

Randy Tei, the vice-president of the franchise that operates the California restaurant said that the Mayorga incident was accidental. The apple juice and the liquor mix were stored in identical plastic bottles, and the manager mistakenly grabbed the wrong container to pour the boy's drink. The company paid the Mayorga's medical bills and offered them free meals as an apology.

Mrs. Mayorga accepted the apology but added, "If they think I'm going back there, they're ridiculous."

QUESTIONS
TO CONSIDER:

■ What is your reaction to this story? Do you believe that the restaurant's explanation for the incident is believable? Why or why not?

■ Sometimes similar-looking containers hold very different contents. Have you ever made a similar mistake? Perhaps you mistook a tube of ointment for a tube of toothpaste or a bottle of lotion for a bottle of shampoo. What would be the results of such a mix-up?

■ The restaurant in the story learned a difficult lesson. Appearances can be deceiving and may not accurately tell us what lies on the inside. We know that the same thing is true about people. Outward appearances do not always match inward character. When appearance matches character, we call that *integrity*. The Bible tells us some signs of personal integrity. Let's discover what they are.

INSTANT **STUDY 22** ■ BIBLE**TRUTHS**

BIBLE TRUTHS

BIBLE**TRUTH** 1

A person of integrity lives by God's Word, not personal desire. TITUS: 2:6

■ **List some occupations that people do not trust. Why do you think that is?**

INSIDE STORY: Contrary to the politically correct crowd, the personal morality of our leaders does matter. The Greek word translated here as "self-controlled" is *sophreneo*. It is used of the Gadarene demoniac in Mark 5:15. Once controlled by demons, this man came under Jesus' control and was proclaimed to be "in his right mind" *(sophreneo)*. A self-controlled person refuses the siren song of Satan and is placed in a righteous state of mind by following the commands of Christ. In Romans 12:3 Paul tells Christians not to be controlled by their inflated egos. We are to compare our behavior to the will of God, exercising "sober judgment" *(sophreneo)*. A self-controlled person never believes that he or she is above God's rule. Finally, Peter tells believers to be clear minded *(sophreneo)*. Why? Because when the Word of God rules someone, he or she is able to effectively pray and await the second coming of Jesus (1 Peter 4:7).

BIBLE**TRUTH** 2

A person of integrity teaches by his or her actions. TITUS 2:7

■ **Sometimes we learn by copying others. What skills have you learned that way?**

INSIDE STORY: A person with integrity serves as an example to others. The Greek word *tupos* comes from a word meaning to be shaped by the striking of a hammer. A metal smith in the ancient world made patterns in that way. The hammer of God's Word shapes a person, making him or her a worthy example to follow. Paul was able to encourage others to follow his example (1 Corinthians 11:1). God has always worked by creating examples. The ark of the covenant in the Old Testament was a "copy" *(tupos)* of something greater in Heaven (Hebrews 8:5). Likewise, a person of integrity models a copy of the character of the Heavenly Father. Paul served as an example *(tupos)* for the Thessalonian Christians, and they served as a model *(tupos)* for Christians in the surrounding regions (2 Thessalonians 3:9; 1 Thessalonians 1:7). Being a worthy pattern to follow is especially important for Christian leaders. Peter tells elders that poor leaders have to rule by forcing compliance. Leaders of integrity lead by being examples *(tupos)* to the flock, not by being taskmasters (1 Peter 5:3).

BIBLE**TRUTH** 3

A person of integrity lives above condemnation. TITUS 2:8

■ **Before some people run for high office, they go through what is called a "vetting process." What do you think that means?**

INSIDE STORY: Paul told Titus that a person of integrity "cannot be condemned" *(akatagnostos)*. Those trying to find fault in a person of integrity will be ashamed of themselves because there will be no substance to the charges (v. 8; 1 Peter 2:15; 3:16).

With integrity we silence our critics. We have a green light from God, power from the Holy Spirit to teach, preach, lead, and be an example. We command respect even from the unsaved. With integrity, we become real Christians—authentic Christians. We become the fragrance of Christ in the world (2 Corinthians 2:14).

The harshest critic of any person, however, is his or her own heart. We can silence even that critic according to John. We can have confidence before God if we know that we follow his commands (1 John 3:19-22).

CHALLENGE Have students to use an A-F grading scale to give themselves an integrity report card. Have them grade their integrity at school, with their family, and with friends. Encourage them to think of ways to raise their grades.

How does God want me to care for my body?

THE BIG TRUTH
TAKING CARE OF OUR BODIES HONORS THE ONE WHO MADE THEM.

CONFIDENTIAL SOURCE:
EXODUS 23:12;
PROVERBS 18:9;
ECCLESIASTES 10:16, 17

Safety First

How healthy are you? What are you doing to protect your health and remain physically fit? Teens' health and fitness is a topic that is often in the news.

Dangerous jobs—A study of nearly 7,000 American teens found that more than half of them have jobs and that 514 (about 7 percent) of them had been injured at work. The researchers have concluded that work-related injuries among youth are a serious health issue.

"Developing programs and strategies to reduce injury must be made a priority," wrote Kristina M. Zierold, assistant professor of family and community medicine at Wake Forest University School of Medicine in Winston-Salem, North Carolina. "Training," she continued, "would emphasize how to identify work-related hazards, how to protect themselves from hazards, and how to address their supervisors with their safety concerns."

Buckle up!—Fewer than half of high school students always use seat belts according to a recent survey by the federal Centers for Disease Control and Prevention. New government data does show a drop in traffic deaths among teen drivers and their teen passengers. But still, unsafe teen driving continues to take a tragic toll.

Teens in Gibson City, Illinois, did something about it. The Harvest Moon Drive-In Theatre in that town showed public service ads produced and performed by local teens that reminded them to buckle up on the ride home. The ads, which also promoted alert and sober driving, were part of a campaign that students at Gibson City-Melvin-Sibley High School, started for a nationwide contest sponsored by State Farm and the National Youth Leadership Council.

Missing shots—Most preschool children get the immunizations required for them. But according to a private health plan study called the Health Plan Employer Data and Information Set, almost a third of teens start school without the needed shots. "Traditionally, people think vaccines are just for young kids," said Maine Immunization Program Director Jiancheng Huang. "It's a lack of knowledge of how bad it (the disease) could be, so they don't take the vaccine."

QUESTIONS TO CONSIDER:

■ Which of the news items above did you find most surprising? Which of the health threats mentioned concerns you the most? Why? In your opinion, what other health concerns threaten teens?

■ In what ways do you attempt to maintain your health and stay physically fit? What are some things you believe you *should* do to take care of your health but you currently do not do?

■ There are a number of ways people seek to maintain their health and stay fit. The Bible, while concerned about our spiritual wellbeing, also has much to say about taking care of our bodies. Let's see what it says.

BIBLE TRUTHS

BIBLE**TRUTH** 1

A healthy diet is necessary for the body to be strengthened. ECCLESIASTES 10:16, 17

■ **An old saying states, "You are what you eat." What does that mean to you?**

INSIDE STORY: In rich cultures overindulgence is common. During Solomon's reign, even the poorest people enjoyed prosperity. As a result, the newly rich were tempted to begin gorging themselves the moment they awoke (Ecclesiastes 10:16). Solomon recommended eating "at a proper time—for strength" (v. 17)!

Overindulgence saps the body of energy. When we "drink too much wine or gorge . . . on meat" the result is "drowsiness" (Proverbs 23:20, 21). In the New Testament, Paul cautioned Titus that the people of Crete were said to be "lazy gluttons" that were more likely to follow false teachers because they lacked the energy to seek truth for themselves (Titus 1:12-14).

Starving oneself is just as unproductive as gluttony. Jonathan's "eyes brightened" when he ate some honey during a grueling military campaign (1 Samuel 14:27, 29, 30). Figs and raisin cakes "revived" an Egyptian slave rescued by David (1 Samuel 30:11, 12). Paul counseled his shipmates to eat in order to survive a shipwreck that lay before them (Acts 27:33, 34).

BIBLE**TRUTH** 2

Proper rest is necessary for the body to be refreshed. EXODUS 23:12

■ **What is a proper amount of sleep for you? How does your body tell you when you have too little or too much?**

INSIDE STORY: The law of Moses required that the people of Israel, their servants, and even animals observe a day of rest so that everyone "may be refreshed" (v. 12). Jesus was sensitive to the need of his disciples to recover from their busy times of ministry (Mark 6:30,

31). David praised God for the rest he grants us—leading us to places of refreshment and rest so that we may be restored (Psalm 23:2, 3).

On the other hand, let us note that God granted one day of rest a week, not three or four! Too much rest can be as destructive as not enough rest. Too much rest can actually sap energy rather than restore it (Proverbs 19:15). One who takes too much time off can end up hungry, have property in ill-repair, or even be enslaved (v. 15; Ecclesiastes 10:18; Proverbs 12:24).

BIBLE**TRUTH** 3

Physical activity is necessary to keep sins in check. PROVERBS 18:9

■ **What is a default setting on a computer? Consider moral choices people make. What are the default settings for those choices?**

INSIDE STORY: If we do not seek physical fitness, our bodies revert to a state of poorer muscle tone and endurance. Solomon taught that choosing not to be active is ultimately choosing to destroy (v. 9). Paul told Timothy, "Workouts in the gymnasium are useful, but a disciplined life in God is far more so, making you fit both today and forever" (1 Timothy 4:8, *The Message*). As fallen human beings, we are "pre-programmed" to default to poor physical and spiritual choices. Becoming aware of that, we must train ourselves to override our natural impulses. We must discipline ourselves physically and spiritually (1 Corinthians 9:27).

CHALLENGE Distribute note cards with the words, diet, rest, and exercise written down the left side of the card. Discuss possible resolutions for each category (e.g., drink no sugared sodas, get eight hours of sleep per night, etc.). Have students complete their own cards with a resolution in each of the three categories.

THE BIG TRUTH

DESTRUCTIVE HABITS KEEP US FROM BEING ALL GOD WANTS US TO BE.

CONFIDENTIAL SOURCE:
PROVERBS 20:1; 31:4, 5;
ROMANS 13:12–14;
EPHESIANS 5:4;
JAMES 1:26

Java Junkies

"It's a comfortable atmosphere, they won't throw you out, your parents aren't there, and it's a good place to chill," comments seventeen-year-old Patricia Eggerton. Like many preteens and teenagers, Patricia has found the local coffee shop a great place to hang out with friends. But many experts are concerned that popular coffee drinks feed unhealthy habits.

One concern is that caffeine is a mood-altering drug, and it doesn't take much to get hooked. Dr. Roland Griffiths of the Johns Hopkins University School of Medicine has found that the caffeine in less than eight ounces of Starbucks® coffee a day can cause addiction. After drinking that amount of coffee three days in a row, one might get headaches, become fatigued, and find it hard to concentrate if he or she goes without the beverage. Sixteen-year-old Kara Murray, an avid coffee drinker, has found this to be true, but notes that most of her friends do not worry about it. Still she cautions, "I feel like it's like cigarettes. You start in high school because it's cool, and you think that after college you'll quit, but then you never do."

Another concern is that coffee drinking may lead to other dangerous habits. Though she loves her coffee drinks, sixteen-year-old Giana Cirolia compares the way adding whipped cream, flavorings, and sugar to mask the bitter taste of coffee with how fruity mixed drinks make it easier for teens to down alcohol. "It's like chocolate milk for big kids," she says. Michele Simon, director of the Center for Informed Food Choices, warns, "You can even think of it [coffee] as a gateway drug." A study by the National Center on Addiction and Substance Abuse at Columbia University found that young women who drink coffee are significantly more likely to become smokers.

Thirdly, doctors worry that teens drink coffee at the exclusion of eating well. Dr. Marcie Beth Schneider, who specializes in adolescent medicine, says that the teens she sees often use coffee to replace a healthy breakfast. "Their No. 1 drink is Starbucks® in the morning. They're not eating there. They're getting coffee." Coffee drinks replace other meals as well. "Think $4," says Giana. "That's what you pay for lunch. Not for coffee *and* lunch. Coffee *is* lunch."

QUESTIONS TO CONSIDER:

■ Do you enjoy hanging out at a coffee shop with friends? Tell why you feel the way you do. How much coffee do you drink in an average week? How concerned are you about the health issues raised by this article? Explain.

■ Name some other habits people have. List some possible destructive results of such habits. Why do you think people pick up such habits, knowing that they may pose very real dangers? What is your worst habit? What negative consequences does it pose for you?

■ God asks us to refrain from habits and practices that may be harmful to us, to those whom we love, and to our relationship with him. Today we are going to look briefly at three bad habits that are common in our world today: drugs, sensuality, and profanity.

INSTANT STUDY 24 ■ BIBLETRUTHS

BIBLE TRUTHS

BIBLE**TRUTH** 1

Substance abuse clouds our judgment.

PROVERBS 20:1; 31:4, 5

■ **Give examples of how drunkenness is portrayed as being humorous. Does your experience teach you something else?**

INSIDE STORY: Drugs give the user a false sense of power while making a fool of him, transforming him from Jekyll to Hyde, from intelligent and caring to stupid and violent (20:1). Even godly men such as Noah and Lot, who stood with God against entire cultures, briefly fell prey to alcohol (Genesis 9:20, 21; 19:30-33). By its very nature addiction is progressive. The need gets greater, and the user wants more.

Drugs themselves are neither good nor bad. Many (including alcohol) have powerful therapeutic value (1 Timothy 5:23). But the misuse of these elements, especially by a leader, will be disastrous (Proverbs 31:4, 5). With all our intelligence and resources, humankind has yet to master the terrible effects of substance abuse.

BIBLE**TRUTH** 2

Sensuality fails to prepare us for eternity.

ROMANS 13:12-14

■ **List specific occasions that require specific clothing. Tell of how someone would look out of place if not dressed properly.**

INSIDE STORY: In Paul's time, Rome offered cultural and business opportunities, arts, and sports. But the dark side of human behavior, evidenced by crime and sexual promiscuity, was also present. Using the imagery of clothing, Paul told the Romans about how to be properly "dressed" to face eternity. Paul exhorted Roman believers to discard the deeds of darkness like old clothes and to put on Christ's armor of light (v. 12). Paul's letter told believers in Rome not to be absorbed in old habits but to don their glittering Christlike garments (v. 14).

The Greek work translated "sexual immorality" is the word *koite*, literally meaning, "bed." The immorality presented today on TV, in movies, in books, and on Internet sites is nothing new. Instead of indiscriminately "bedding" *(koite),* believers in Paul's day, like us, were called to model lasting relationships, seeing "the marriage bed *(koite)* kept pure" (Hebrews 13:4). Debauchery is excessive indulgence in sensual pleasures—or in present-day language, "partying." Such me-first, no-holds-barred behaviors produce anxiety and jealousy. Nothing good will come of it (Romans 13:13).

BIBLE**TRUTH** 3

Vulgar speech turns our focus from God.

EPHESIANS 5:4; JAMES 1:26

■ **Has someone you once admired ever shocked you by something he or she said? Tell about that time.**

INSIDE STORY: Vulgar speech includes cursing others, coarse jokes, speaking ill of others, and demeaning ourselves. Paul calls these types of vulgarity "out of place" in the believer's life (Ephesians 5:4). Foul speech labels a person as one who does not care about having a relationship with Christ.

Perverse language can be carried undetected like a concealed weapon into any home, marketplace, or church, where it can do a world of damage. James tells us what we already instinctively know. A person can claim religion and even perform acts of service in the name of God. But reckless speech from that person will lower him in the eyes of others, making religious claims and actions appear worthless (James 1:26).

CHALLENGE Help your students to memorize 1 Corinthians 10:13—the promise that God will provide a way out of any temptation and the temptation will never be more than we can bear. You may choose to have your students memorize this Scripture by reciting it, acting it out, or drawing symbols to represent it.

Are my feelings valid?

Unfortunate Outbursts

Former secretary of state Colin Powell once remarked, "Get mad, then get over it." The news from around the world is filled with stories of people who only took *half* of this advice.

Dogged Determination—Tammy McCarty went to Ouachita Parish [Louisiana] Animal Shelter and asked for a dog. When the police officer working security at the pound told her she would have to pay adoption fees for the animal, McCarty punched him in his face and head. McCarty then fled the animal shelter with her new pet, pursued by sheriff's deputies. Later, when deputies tried to handcuff her, McCarty struck a deputy in the ribs. Taken to the Ouachita Correctional Center, McCarty tried to hit another deputy and grabbed another, despite being shot twice with an officer's stun gun. She was charged with simple battery of a police officer, resisting an officer, aggravated assault of a police officer, and vehicle trespassing. Bond was set at $11,000—much more than pet adoption fees!

Not Helping His Case—Ignacio Javier Bilbao Goikoetxea was on trial in Madrid, Spain. He was charged with threatening Judge Baltasar Garzon at an earlier trial. As Garzon testified against Goikoetxea, the defendant kicked the bulletproof screen surrounding the bench and screamed obscenities at the witness. "If you're a man, come here . . . I'm going to skin you alive . . . I look forward to shooting you seven times when I get my hands on you," he shouted. "I believe in the armed struggle. I will continue with the armed fight until I die or I'm killed," Goikoetxea continued. It is the second time he has been tried for threatening Garzon after being jailed for two years at a previous trial.

So Much for the Coach of the Year Award—Cory Petero, assistant coach of a junior high football team, got a little too involved in the game. When a player from the opposing team made a late hit on Petero's son, the coach rushed onto the field and assaulted the offending thirteen-year-old player. This action sparked a brawl that lasted for about twenty minutes and involved parents and children from both teams. Petero turned himself in to Stockton [California] police after the game. Reg Evans, vice president of the Delta Youth Football League, said Petero was out of line and should be banned from coaching.

Not Camera Shy—"Speed cameras" designed to film motorists breaking traffic laws in Manchester, England, caught Craig Moore driving too fast. In an attempt to destroy the evidence, Moore stole some explosive materials from his workplace and blew up the camera. Unfortunately for Moore, the camera survived the blast and recorded his crime. He is now serving a four-month jail sentence.

QUESTIONS TO CONSIDER:

■ Look at each of the stories above. What made each of the people angry? Was anger an appropriate emotion in any or all of these situations? Explain. How did acting on their emotions make each situation worse?

■ Recall a time in which circumstances caused you to become very emotional. Did you let your feelings overrule good judgment? Tell about it.

■ Our emotions can be a measure of what's happening to us, but we must not allow our emotions to control our lives. Today we'll learn a three-step strategy for taking charge of our emotions.

INSTANT **STUDY 25** ■ BIBLE**TRUTHS**

BIBLE**TRUTH** 1

Don't compare yourself to others. PSALM 73:2, 3

■ **What does it mean to try to "keep up with the Joneses"? Why can that lead to depression?**

INSIDE STORY: Asaph, the author of Psalm 73, was the leader of one of David's temple choirs. In this psalm he shared his experience of depression and showed what caused it. First Asaph confessed that his "feet had almost slipped…when I saw the prosperity of the wicked" (vv. 2, 3). It is easy to look at others and think that we are more worthy of God's blessings than others who have them or that God allows and possibly even rewards sinfulness. The facts are that all are equally unworthy of God's grace and that sin has inescapable consequences (Romans 3:23; Galatians 6:7). Uncontrolled envy is seen clearly in the account of Sarai, wife of Abram. At her urging, Abram fathered an heir through Sarai's servant Hagar (Genesis 16:1-3). When Hagar became pregnant, however, Sarai sensed that Hagar felt superior to her and conflict began to grow (v. 4). As emotions ran high, Sarai blamed Abram for her suffering and abused her servant (vv. 5, 6).

BIBLE**TRUTH** 2

Refuse to feel sorry for yourself. PSALM 73:13-17

■ **Tell about the last time you held a personal "pity party?" Looking back, was your self-pity justified? Explain.**

INSIDE STORY: Uncontrolled emotion led Asaph into self-pity. "I've been stupid to play by the rules; what has it gotten me? A long run of bad luck, that's what—a slap in the face every time I walk out the door. (Psalm 73:13, 14, *The Message*). His emotions overrode his intellect (vv. 15, 16). Emotions turned Asaph into a whiner!

The prophet Jonah's emotions led him to pity himself. After the people of Nineveh repented and God withdrew his promised judgment, Jonah doubted whether everything he had been through was worth it. He even commanded God to take his life (Jonah 4:1-3)! In his mind, it was all about Jonah!

When our emotions cause us to look inward and wallow in our pain, we blind ourselves to truth. Asaph "entered the sanctuary of God . . . [where he] saw the whole picture" (Psalm 73:17, *The Message*). God illustrated Jonah's pettiness to him with a vine God caused to grow (Jonah 4:4-11). When we feel sorry for ourselves, we need to remember that even the gates of Hell cannot prevail against God's chosen (Matthew 16:18).

BIBLE**TRUTH** 3

Surrender more fully to God. PSALM 73:25, 26

■ **How does trust in an all-powerful God enable us to override our emotions?**

INSIDE STORY: Asaph finally controlled his emotions by surrendering his envy and self-pity and embracing hope offered by God. He admitted to himself that no matter what he had on earth, it would mean nothing if God were not with him (v. 25). By God's power he could remain emotionally stable (v. 26).

The apostle Paul was imprisoned in Rome awaiting trial. Some Christians distanced themselves from him. But Paul recognized that his unjust imprisonment allowed him to effectively minister to his captors, and the controversy over his imprisonment allowed even those embarrassed by him to win a hearing from unbelievers (Philippians 1:12-18). Paul concluded that God could take even injustice and bring good from it (vv. 20, 21).

CHALLENGE Play emotion charades. Have students portray an emotion with facial expressions only, and ask the rest of the group to guess the emotion. Then discuss how the Bible lesson addresses each emotion.

make me such a failure? Why did God

Voter Revolt

In 2006, British prime minister Tony Blair suffered a humiliating defeat. Although Blair was not running in the elections, the sound thrashing received by his political party was seen as a reaction to his policies and scandals in his administration. Blair's Labor Party received only 26 percent of the votes in local council elections, while the opposing Conservative party received 40 percent. The remaining council seats were divided among smaller parties such as the leftist Liberal Democrats and the right-wing British National Party. This was the Labor Party's worst defeat in almost ten years.

After the election, prime minister Blair took strong action and drastically reshuffled his government. Blair demoted Foreign Secretary Jack Straw, a figure closely tied to an unpopular war in Iraq and a close friend of his American counterpart, U. S. Secretary of State Condoleezza Rice. Straw became the leader of the House of Commons, a position of lesser power.

Blair also stripped power from his deputy prime minister, John Prescott. Prescott had admitted an extramarital affair with his secretary. Furthermore, Blair fired home secretary Charles Clarke, roughly the equivalent of the U.S. attorney general. Clarke was under fire for a scandal involving illegal immigrants in his country. Critics charged that under Clarke's watch over 1,000 foreigners who were in British prisons were recently released into the general population rather than being deported.

Nevertheless, Blair's remedies failed to satisfy his enemies or allies. Conservative Party leader David Cameron told reporters: "It will take more than a reshuffle. What we need in this country is a replacement." A member of Blair's own party agreed. "There really is a need for change right at the top now," said Geraldine Smith, a Labor Party member of Parliament. "The change that many people would like to see is actually Tony Blair announcing when he is going to stand down and have a proper timetable and an orderly transition of power." Blair had been in office since 1997 and wasn't up for reelection until 2010.

At first, Blair refused to step down as prime minister. "To state a timetable would simply paralyze the proper working of government, put at risk the necessary changes we are making for Britain and therefore damage the country. It wouldn't end this distraction but merely take it to a new level," Blair announced. Under pressure from his own party, however, Blair stepped down in June of 2007.

QUESTIONS
TO CONSIDER:

■ List some of the failures for which British prime minister Tony Blair was blamed. Which of these do you consider the largest failures? Why? What are some failures of other famous political leaders of the past or present? How have people reacted to those failures? How did Blair react to defeat? Do you believe that his actions were right or wrong? Explain.

■ Think of a time when you suffered a humiliating defeat. How did you react? How would you have acted differently if the same thing were to happen today?

■ We have all faced times during which our plans have failed and we have felt defeated. Today we will see the steps an important biblical leader took to overcome failure.

INSTANT **STUDY 26** ■ **BIBLETRUTHS**

57

BIBLE TRUTHS

BIBLE**TRUTH** 1

When you feel helpless, seek God for direction.
1 SAMUEL 30:1-8

■ **Jesus talked about "the blind leading the blind." What is the alternative to getting advice from those who know as little as you?**

INSIDE STORY: King Saul had made attempts to kill David, who had already been anointed to be the next king (16:13; 18:10-12). The prophet Gad had told David to escape Saul by going to Judah, but David took his 600 fighting men and their families into Philistine territory (22:5; 27:1). David feigned allegiance to King Achish of the Philistines, who gave David, his men, and their families the city of Ziklag as a base. David and his men pretended to sack the villages of neighboring Israelites, while actually attacking ruthless, godless Amalekites (vv. 5-12).

This plan backfired. When David and his men returned to Ziklag, they found their town burned to the ground and their women and children gone. They suspected Amalekite raiders, the very people David had attacked to impress and deceive King Achish (30:1-6). Following his own instincts and ignoring the counsel of God had caused David to fail. But "David found strength in the LORD his God" (v. 6).

David requested God's presence and counsel. God's answer rang with power and assurance: "Pursue them…You will certainly overtake them and succeed in the rescue" (v. 8).

BIBLE**TRUTH** 2

When you feel like giving up, press on.
1 SAMUEL 30:9, 10

■ **Coaches always seem to say, "No pain, no gain." Tell about a time when you saw some truth in that.**

INSIDE STORY: The word of the Lord gave David the courage to go after the Amalekites. David's men quickly regained their faith in him and his message of victory from the Lord. All the men went with him as far as the Besor Ravine. There, a third of the troops—too weak to go on—were left to recover. David did not push them beyond their capabilities, even in this emergency, for God had assured success. Surely David too was exhausted, but he continued on (vv. 9, 10). To conquer failure, David trusted God's power—not his own—and didn't quit.

BIBLE**TRUTH** 3

When you feel like lashing out, make friends.
1 SAMUEL 30:11-15

■ **How does a bad mood cause you to react to others sometimes? Why is that counterproductive?**

INSIDE STORY: David's compassion for his men stands in contrast to an unnamed Amalekite raider who had left his sick Egyptian slave in a field to die. The slave was a foreigner, servant of the enemy. But David took pity, fed him, and made him an ally (vv. 11, 12). The meeting was more than luck. In exchange for protection the slave offered critical information about the raiding party's location. The slave said, "swear to me before God," indicating that he was also a believer in the one and only God (v. 15). Providence was at work, forging a friendship between king and slave to save a whole town. To conquer failure David trusted God and made friends with a fellow believer.

CHALLENGE

Toss a football to a student and ask him or her to share one task that had once brought defeat but is now ready to be tackled again. As time permits, let each student to whom the ball is tossed give practical advice and encourage one another to press on.

THE BIG TRUTH

LET'S SEEK GOD'S WISDOM IN MANAGING OUR MOMENTS.

CONFIDENTIAL SOURCE:
ECCLESIASTES 11:9; 12:1;
JOHN 9:4

Sofa Spuds

Many people spent New Year's Day of 2007 watching sports on television. But four Chicago-area fans were trying to make this activity pay off for them.

The fifth annual Ultimate Couch Potato contest began at 10 AM on New Year's Day at Chicago's ESPN Zone sports bar. Four contestants (who were chosen by submitting 200-word essays) competed for about $5,000 in prizes including an Olevia® 42" LCD HDTV and a Dreamseat® sports-themed recliner.

Back in the competition was the 2006 champ, Jason Pisarik, an accountant from Lombard, Illinois. Pisarik was glued to the tube for thirty consecutive hours the year before to win that title. Area teen, Jimmy Harding, was one of Pisarik's challengers. "I think I have a good chance," Harding said before the contest. "I've stayed up for two days straight before."

Stacy Gleason, a mother of three, was the only woman in the competition. Somewhat concerned that household chores would not get done in her absence, the paralegal from Indiana said, "I don't know how guys do it." Nevertheless she put thoughts of cooking and cleaning behind her to achieve a higher goal. "I'm doing this for girls everywhere who don't get to do this while their husbands morph into the furniture watching sports on TV," she quipped.

Jimmy Harding was especially concerned about having only a five-minute bathroom break every hour. He planned to "try and drink enough caffeine to stay awake, but eat as close as I can to the eight-hour point" (when he would get an additional fifteen-minute break).

The contestants were excited about the competition. "I couldn't think of anything better than to sit and watch a bunch of games and get served food and drink all day," said Pisarik. Of course, even a good thing could get tiresome after doing it for hours.

Nevertheless, nearly forty hours into the contest, Pisarik's eyes were still glued to the screen. His only remaining challenger, graduate student, Noah Manly, conceded. Pisarik won his second straight title, but failed to set the world record of sixty-nine hours and forty-eight minutes of consecutive TV viewing. That record was set in New York City in September 2005 by Canadian Suresh Joachim.

QUESTIONS
TO CONSIDER:

■ Would you like to have the opportunity to compete in a contest like this? Why or why not? How would you prepare for it? What would be your strategy for winning it?

■ Could people label you a "couch potato"? Why or why not? What is the longest time that you have spent doing nothing but watching TV? What are some other activities that take up a lot of your time? What would you do if only you had more time?

■ We may not watch sports for two days without sleep, but there are many other activities that take our time. The Bible clearly says that time does not come in unlimited supply for human beings. The time we spend is gone forever. Let's see what the Bible says about using that time wisely.

BIBLE TRUTHS

BIBLE**TRUTH** 1

Take time to enjoy life. ECCLESIASTES 11:9

■ **Do you know any workaholics? Why do you agree or disagree with their choices concerning work and play?**

INSIDE STORY: King Solomon encouraged every believer to look at the days he or she is given and "enjoy them all" (v. 8). Enjoying life "is a gift of God" (5:19). In the New Testament James tells us, "Every good and perfect gift is from above," and Paul agreed that God "richly provides us with everything for our enjoyment" (James 1:17; 1 Timothy 6:17). God wants Christians to enjoy life, not try to avoid or to merely endure life.

Yet there is a difference between enjoying life as a gift from God and seeing personal pleasure as a god. Paul warned against those whose "god is their stomach", and Peter called those who sought only pleasure "an accursed brood" (Philippians 3:19; 2 Peter 2:14). Solomon, while wanting us to "be happy" and to "follow the ways of [our] heart and whatever [our] eyes see," reminded believers that we are all still subject to God's standards of righteousness (Ecclesiastes 11:9). Pleasure is *not* forbidden to the Christian, but misusing or idolizing God's gifts intended for our pleasure is.

BIBLE**TRUTH** 2

Do not put off having a relationship with God.
ECCLESIASTES 12:1

■ **Some think that Christianity is just for the very young and the elderly. Why do you suppose they think that way?**

INSIDE STORY: Solomon believed that all of the activities available to us when we are young make us feel that we just don't have time for God. For that reason, the wise king commanded, "Remember your Creator in the days of your youth" (v. 1). A psalmist expressed this idea when singing, "Better is one day in your courts than a thousand elsewhere" (Psalm 84:10). Moses wrote that we must recognize that the

best we can hope for is seventy or eighty years of life on this earth, and those years are gone before we know it (90:10). But if we "number our days aright" by knowing God, we will gain wisdom that has eternal consequences (v. 12). When writing to the Corinthians years later, Paul encouraged them not to put off seeking God. "Now is the time of God's favor, now is the day of salvation" (2 Corinthians 6:2). We are also to encourage others to remember God now, "as long as it is called Today" (Hebrews 3:13).

BIBLE **TRUTH** 3

Invest your time in doing God's work. JOHN 9:4

■ **List some things people believe give their life purpose. With which do you agree and with which do you disagree? Why?**

INSIDE STORY: As Jesus prepared to heal a man born blind (v. 4), he spoke of the daylight and nighttime in all men's lives. Daylight was the only time in ancient Palestine when men could work their fields. But Jesus was talking about more than just farming. In his lesson *day* represented a man's available life and *night* represented his death. Jesus' own death would come shortly, so he was eager to do the work of his Father in the little time he had left (v. 5). The lesson is for all of his disciples, because Jesus said "we" must work to serve the Father. Most of these apostles would be cut down in the prime of their lives; only John would live to old age. Whether their remaining years were long or short, the point was to use every bit of their time for God (Ephesians 5:16). As King Solomon said, "Whatever your hand finds to do, do it with all your might, for in the grave, where you are going, there is neither working nor planning nor knowledge nor wisdom" (Ecclesiastes 9:10).

CHALLENGE
Give each student one adhesive color dot (available in the stationery department of most stores) and a pen. Have them decide whether they need to find time for constructive fun (F), meaningful worship (W), or acts of service to others (S) in their schedules for this week. Have them write an F, W, or S on their dot to remind them of their choices. Then have each student place that dot on the face of his or her watch.

SERIOUS STUDY BRINGS BLESSINGS FROM GOD.

CONFIDENTIAL SOURCE: PROVERBS 1:1–7

Why should I study?

Back to School

Mid-August seems to come far too fast! Although back-to-school time arrives too quickly for many, going back to school means something different to different people.

Many parents and teachers see the need to prepare students for the transition from vacation to the much more structured routine school requires. Angie Hubler, a sixth grade teacher from Indiana tries to get her own children ready for school. "We're trying to do the beach one day, then go to work in my classroom the next day," she said. "We're still on break; it's too nice; they wanna play; they don't wanna focus on school." Hubler tries to prepare her children by adding some academic discipline to the last days of vacation. "Bedtime is always a time when we do thirty minutes of story time. The morning is a good time to do a little journaling or work on some flash cards," she said.

The business world, however, sees back-to-school time as an important selling season. In July Wal-Mart usually prepares for shoppers by reducing prices on thousands of items. If other retailers are going to compete, they have to try to beat or match Wal-Mart's prices. A few years ago, a shopping cart full of back-to-school items cost $71.68 at Wal-Mart on July 17. The same items cost $77.71 at Target. A week later, Target charged $73.56 for those same supplies, but Wal-Mart dropped their price to $69.30. These price wars are necessary because the need for these purchases must be balanced with the typical family's need to watch the budget. "Parents are trying to cut back spending wherever they can as the money pinch tightens this year," said Britt Beemer, chairman of America's Research Group.

Some students, especially fashion-conscious females, see back-to-school as a time to show off the latest fashions. "I want a tote bag by Jaye Hersh that the celebrities are wearing; they're called *Market Bags*," said seventeen-year-old Krissy Stern, who lives in Bronxville, New York. "It's more stylish than a backpack." Actresses Reese Witherspoon and Jessica Alba have been photographed sporting these $100+ monogrammed bags. Sixteen-year-old Lydia Stover cites Nicole Richie as someone whose style she admires. "Sometimes I'll look at what celebrities are wearing, and think 'Oh, that's a cute outfit' and recreate it somehow," she said. Jacqueline Nasser, *ELLEgirl* Fashion Market Editor, said teens take a cue from shows like *Laguna Beach*, *The O.C.*, *The Hills*, and *My Super Sweet 16* that portray a certain lifestyle. "They have been surrounded by celebrities and TV programs where fashion is the central point," she said.

QUESTIONS TO CONSIDER:

■ List some of the attitudes about the back-to-school season that you find in the preceding article. How does this season make you feel? How are you preparing for your return to school?

■ Now let's consider attitudes toward school in general. What is your attitude toward school? Explain why you feel that way. To what extent do your friends share those feelings? Why do you think many students are negative toward school? What is the value of going to school, in your opinion?

■ Parents, teachers, students, and storeowners may all see going back to school in different ways. In thinking about school as a time to sell notebooks, a time to get the kids out of the house, or a time to impress one's peers with designer accessories, a big question may be left unanswered—"Why bother with learning anyway?" Let's see what the Bible has to say about that.

BIBLE TRUTHS

BIBLE**TRUTH** 1

We study to keep from being led astray by our sinful nature. PROVERBS 1:1-4

■ **Imagine playing a sport without having studied the rules. What might result?**

INSIDE STORY: From the very beginning, sin has had its roots in our minds. When the serpent first tempted Eve in the Garden, he began by questioning what she knew about God and God's Word (Genesis 3:1). Paul stated that sin has made our thinking futile (Romans 1:21). But God-given wisdom works with that corrupted mind. Paul told us that we can be transformed by the renewing of our minds (12:2). In Psalm 119:9, the writer asks, "How can a young man keep his way pure?" The answer is "By living according to your word." Study has value because it is the first step in "acquiring a disciplined and prudent life" (Proverbs 1:3). It is useful to note that the Holy Spirit often works in our minds. The grace of God delivered by the Spirit can lead to repentance, literally a change of direction caused by a change of mind (Romans 2:4). The Spirit works with our minds to build convictions—belief and commitment to God and his Word (1 Thessalonians 1:5). The Spirit also develops a conscience within our minds that works to keep us from wandering astray from God's Word (Romans 9:1). A mind that is trained to evaluate and overrule emotion and instinct helps us in every area of life.

BIBLE**TRUTH** 2

We study to find ways to put our knowledge to practical use. PROVERBS 1:5, 6

■ **Share the most useless fact you know. What makes it useless?**

INSIDE STORY: Many students ask the question, "When am I ever going to use this?" Knowing facts without using those facts is useless. Solomon agrees that knowing facts is important, but more is necessary. Study begins with knowing facts. Then more study allows "the wise . . .[to] add to their learning, and let the discerning get guidance" (v. 5).

The second reason to study is to find ways to put previously acquired knowledge to practical use. Educators call this step of learning "application." Perhaps we learn Scriptures for points at camp or in Bible school, but then we quickly forget them because we don't fully understand why we need to know them. Bible knowledge must be used in the practical exercise of everyday living.

BIBLE**TRUTH** 3

We study because we know that God is the source of all truth. PROVERBS 1:7

■ **Bible scholars talk about *natural revelation* and *special revelation* from God. What do you suppose those terms mean?**

INSIDE STORY: Students in a Bible class understand that the truths they are studying come from God. But the same is true of what is learned in school. Since God is "the Maker of heaven and earth, the sea, and everything in them" (Psalm 146:6), the truths of this world—science, math, language, biology, and more—are just as much God's truths as the Bible itself. "The heavens declare the glory of God; the skies proclaim the work of his hands" (19:1). "For since the creation of the world God's invisible qualities—his eternal power and divine nature—have been clearly seen, being understood from what has been made" (Romans 1:20).

Study helps us discipline ourselves by learning facts. But finally, study draws us closer to the one who is "the beginning of knowledge" (Proverbs 1:7). When all of the facts are put together, we begin to recognize that there is someone who is the author of all of those facts. The Bible refers to this as "hiding" or "treasuring and pondering" information in one's heart (Psalm 119:11; Luke 2:19, 51). Study helps point us toward God.

CHALLENGE Have a commissioning service with your group at back-to-school time, dedicating it to God's service.

INSTANT **STUDY** 28 . . . CONTINUED

THE BIG TRUTH
GODLY ATTITUDES AND ACTIONS CAUSE COMMUNITIES TO TAKE NOTICE.

CONFIDENTIAL SOURCE:
LEVITICUS 19:32-34;
MATTHEW 5:13-16;
1 THESSALONIANS 4:11, 12;
1 PETER 2:17

Bridging the Gap

During rush hour on August 1, 2007, the I-35W bridge over the Mississippi River in Minneapolis collapsed, hurtling cars into the water below. This tragedy was met with acts of bravery and kindness that continued weeks later.

Visitor Turned Rescuer

Joe Reed gave assistance to a community where he didn't even live. Reed lived in Tennessee and worked as assistant director of the Rutherford County Emergency Management Agency. He was in Minneapolis for a conference on Homeland Security. Because the hotel where the conference was being held was booked, Reed ended up staying in a hotel with a view of the Interstate 35W bridge. "I guess I was supposed to be there," Reed said. He went on to explain that by coincidence he was looking out his hotel window when the bridge collapsed. Immediately, Reed went out to see what happened, and he saw many lives in danger. Not thinking twice, Reed put his training into action, pulling one woman out of the water and helping children escape from a bus.

People from Minnesota called Murfreesboro, Tennessee, to thank Reed and praise him as a "big hero." Roger Allen, Reed's boss, said Reed was a "true public servant." Reed humbly responded, "It's what being an American is all about."

Local Student Rewarded

For twenty-year-old Jeremy Hernandez, his Minneapolis community gave back to him in honor of his rescue efforts. When the Minneapolis bridge collapsed, Hernandez was on a bus caring for dozens of children who were on a field trip. The collapse caused the bus to get jammed into a guardrail.

Hernandez forced open the back door of the bus and helped the children get off safely. CNN interviewed Hernandez, and somewhere in the questioning Hernandez revealed that he was a former student of Dunwoody College of Technology in Minneapolis. Hernandez went to school for a semester for the auto mechanics program, he explained, but he had to quit because of financial strain.

Many people in the community flooded the college with calls, saying they'd like to assist Hernandez in getting back to school. The Dunwoody president, Ben Wright, had seen Hernandez on CNN and his heart went out to him as well. Between community donations and the school's own generosity, a scholarship was been set up for Hernandez to return to classes.

QUESTIONS
TO CONSIDER:

■ The Minneapolis community was obviously thankful for the difference Reed and Hernandez made in the lives of its citizens. How do you feel after reading about these two men? What other examples have you heard of, both in the Minnesota tragedy and in other catastrophes, where people heroically assisted others in need?

■ Reading stories such as these or simply looking around our world and seeing the needs that exist, we can be inspired to find a way to make a difference. What difference would you like to make in your community?

■ Making a difference in our community is a responsibility we all have as Christians. Let's look at three roles God expects us to play in our communities.

BIBLE TRUTHS

BIBLE **TRUTH** 1

We are commanded to work so that we will not be a burden to others. 1 THESSALONIANS 4:11, 12

■ **An old saying tells us, "Idle hands are the tools of the Devil." Tell why you agree or disagree.**

INSIDE STORY: Paul urged the Christians in Thessalonica to make a difference in their society by living quiet, industrious lives (vv. 11, 12). Quiet, hard-working Christians will win the respect of others. People of the world will inwardly admire us because of our decency, our work ethic, and our self-sufficiency. Paul also described those who "are not busy; they are busybodies" (2 Thessalonians 3:11). Those who are not engaged in constructive work often busy themselves destructively.

The Bible has many stories of people making real contributions to their society before they reached adulthood. Miriam saved her baby brother Moses from execution (Exodus 2:1-10). A servant girl brought an army commander to a prophet who could heal him (2 Kings 5:1-14). A young man provided food that would be used to feed a multitude (John 6:1-15).

BIBLE**TRUTH** 2

We are called to show respect and cooperate with others in our communities.

LEVITICUS 19:32-34; 1 PETER 2:17

■ **How might a driver react to another driver with a Christian bumper sticker that recklessly speeds by him on the highway?**

INSIDE STORY: The apostle Peter urged believers to make a difference in their communities by being good citizens (1 Peter 2:17). Peter had said that they should obey the rules established by people in authority, realizing that those people are sent by God to punish wrongdoers (vv. 13, 14). Most of all, Christians should learn to show proper respect and honor (v. 17). Even though their fellow citizens were pagan unbelievers, Christians were to treat them with respect. Even though the emperor at that time was Nero, Christians were to honor him as their king.

A principle from the Old Testament expands upon that principle of respect and cooperation. Rather than treating old people with scorn as if they were outdated and irrelevant, Moses told younger people to stand up when an older person entered the room and to show respect for the elderly (Leviticus 19:32). Also, tolerance for people of different racial and ethnic backgrounds is included in the following verses (vv. 33, 34).

BIBLE**TRUTH** 3

We are called to be representatives of God in our communities. MATTHEW 5:13-16

■ **If your church were totally gone from your community tomorrow, how would it be missed?**

INSIDE STORY: Jesus said his disciples were the salt of the earth (v. 13). In the first century salt was such a valuable commodity that it was an essential part of a Roman soldier's pay. (Our word "salary" actually comes from the Latin word for "salt.") Salt was not only desirable for making food taste better; it was also the only way they had to keep meat from spoiling. Christians, then, make the world more palatable to God and their presence helps to retard the world's tendency to become more corrupt.

Similarly, the Christian's influence in society is like light (v. 14). In a dark and depraved world Christians shine brightly like the stars (Philippians 2:15). But what good is a light if it is covered up—or burnt out? If a light is not seen, what good is it doing (Matthew 5:15)? The basis of that witness is a life of good works, a life that earns the respect of others and causes them to praise God (v. 16).

CHALLENGE Take a few minutes to brainstorm ways your students can become change agents in their communities, both individually and collectively. Encourage students to write down some ideas and investigate them this week.

INSTANT **STUDY** 29 . . . CONTINUED

CONFIDENTIAL SOURCE:
JOSHUA 1:1-7

Does God have a special purpose for me?

Officer Elvis

On January 8 of each year, people all over the world celebrate the birthday of Elvis Aron Presley. Probably one of the most unusual places that has recognized Elvis' birthday was the Richard Nixon Presidential Library & Birthplace.

The King of Rock and Roll has become a role model for many. It has been estimated that there are more that 85,000 Elvis impersonators in the world today! Many want to be Elvis when they grow up. But Presley himself had other career ambitions.

Elvis Presley had a fascination with a career in law enforcement. This led to a secret meeting between him and President Nixon on December 21, 1970. Artifacts from that historic meeting were on display at the Nixon Library to celebrate the King's birthday.

Earlier in 1970 Presley wrote to J. Edgar Hoover requesting to join the FBI to fight drug abuse and Communism. Having his request denied, Elvis took decisive action—he made a surprise visit to the White House. Upon Presley's arrival in a stretch limousine, one of his bodyguards handed over a letter from Elvis addressed to Nixon requesting a meeting. "I will be here as long as it takes to get the credentials of a Federal Agent," reads the letter in part. "I have done an in-depth study of drug abuse and Communist brainwashing techniques and I am right in the middle of the whole thing where I can and will do the most good."

Less than three hours after his arrival, Presley was led into the Oval Office. During the meeting, Elvis showed the President his collection of police badges from around the country. He renewed his request for a badge from the U.S. Bureau of Narcotics and Dangerous Drugs, recognizing him as a federal agent at large. Although the chief of the narcotics bureau had refused to make Elvis a deputy, Nixon overruled that decision and gave Presley a badge.

A picture of Elvis Presley and Richard Nixon taken at that meeting is the most requested photo from the National Archives. The same photo adorns T-shirts, cups, notepads, and watches for sale at the Richard Nixon Library & Birthplace gift shop.

"The two of them together somehow is almost incomprehensible," said Bud Krogh, Nixon's former staff member who set up the meeting on that day. "The King of Rock and the president of the United States shaking hands in the Oval Office doesn't compute for a lot of people."

QUESTIONS TO CONSIDER:

■ Why is it "almost incomprehensible" to many that a rock star would want to be a law enforcement officer? Why do you think Elvis wanted to hold such a position?

■ What are your future career plans? What job would you like to hold someday? How do you plan to become qualified for such a career?

■ Although Elvis wanted to be a federal agent, he did not have the training to do so. We may have ideas for a dream job that we might like to hold someday. But the Bible tells us that Christians have an even greater calling. Let's see what the Bible says is necessary for success in God's service.

BIBLE TRUTHS

BIBLE**TRUTH** 1

Remember the lessons of your teachers.

JOSHUA 1:1-3

■ **Who is the best teacher you ever had? How do you still apply what you learned from him or her?**

INSIDE STORY: Moses led the children of Israel out of Egypt and to the edge of the promised land. Along the way, his aide Joshua watched, helped, and learned. On Moses' passing, the mantle of leadership fell to Joshua. Hundreds of thousands of men, women, and children were about to cross the Jordan as a conquering army, but these people were not experienced and disciplined, but willful and stubborn (Exodus 34:9; Deuteronomy 10:16; 31:27).

The first thing Joshua did was to send orders through his commanders to the people to prepare to march (Joshua 1:10, 11). Then he told a select group of people, "Remember the command that Moses . . . gave you" (v. 13). Now that his teacher was gone, he ordered others to remember the lessons Moses taught.

In the New Testament, the relationship of Paul and Timothy is similar to that of Moses and Joshua. Paul commanded his son in the faith to remember his lessons, who taught them, and from where those lessons came (2 Timothy 3:14, 15).

BIBLE**TRUTH** 2

Understand your goal. JOSHUA 1:4

■ **It is said, "If you don't know where you are going, any road will get you there." React to that statement.**

INSIDE STORY: God gave Joshua a clear goal: "Your territory will extend from the desert to Lebanon, and from the great river, the Euphrates—all the Hittite country—to the Great Sea on the west" (v. 4). Joshua clearly understood the goal and sent spies into the area to have a detailed look at the task God had set before him (Joshua 2:1).

God is the ultimate goal-setter. After his resurrection, Jesus gathered his disciples and gave them a goal for both them and all of us who would follow. We call that goal of going into the world to win others to Christ the Great Commission (Matthew 28:18-20). Christians know that our ultimate personal goal—eternal life with our Lord—is attained by Christ's work and not our own. But he does allow us to choose between many courses and options in life. He also expects us to always stay at his side while we do so.

BIBLE**TRUTH** 3

Trust in God for protection. JOSHUA 1:5-7

■ **Imagine how you feel hiking in an unfamiliar forest alone. Now contrast that with how you would feel with an experienced guide by your side.**

INSIDE STORY: God promised Joshua his complete protection as Joshua's perfect bodyguard, never leaving his side (v. 5). Joshua was told to carefully obey the law Moses had passed on to him (v. 7). Within seven years Joshua gained control of the promised land. Though more areas remained, essentially the victory was won and the land was divided among the tribes of Israel. The names of the vanquished kings are listed in Joshua 12.

Christians today can continue to march confidently through life. After all, God gives us "a spirit of power" (2 Timothy 1:7). We can know that the God we serve is "greater than the one who is in the world" (1 John 4:4).

CHALLENGE

Before your session, create three signs with the following titles: *Recall, Realize, Rely.* Place these signs in three different prayer stations in the room. Divide students into three groups, sending each group to a different station where they will ask God for that one specific characteristic of Joshua on that sign. Rotate groups so all students spend time in each station.

Has my dysfunctional family warped me for life?

Fugitive Prince

C. S. Lewis's *The Chronicles of Narnia: Prince Caspian* is a popular book and became a successful motion picture. Like many heroes, Caspian overcame some great obstacles. The same was true of Caspian's creator.

In Lewis's classic tale, Caspian's parents died when he was young. His villainous Uncle Miraz became his guardian. In the opening minutes of the film version of the story, Miraz seeks to murder his nephew in order to usurp the throne.

Ben Barnes, who played the heroic prince, told reporters, "Caspian is an earnest character. He's a bit of a lost soul." Barnes continued to explain, "Caspian hasn't been parented and has been brought up by someone who essentially doesn't care about him at all and is just waiting to have his own heir so he can get rid of him. That's not a very loving environment to be brought up in. The closest thing he has is his professor, and that was probably only a couple of years."

In some ways, the crises in the life of Caspian mirrored some of the hardships in Lewis's own life. When he was only ten, his mother died of cancer, leaving him to be reared by his distant, demanding, and eccentric father. That same year, Lewis was sent off to the Wynyard School in Watford, Hertfordshire. The atmosphere of the school was oppressive. Shortly after Lewis's enrollment, the school was closed and the headmaster, Robert "Oldie" Capron, was committed to an insane asylum.

At the age of nineteen, Lewis enlisted in the British Army and experienced brutal trench warfare during World War I. On April 15, 1917, Lewis was wounded during the Battle of Arras. He recovered, but he would later lose his best friend, "Paddy" Moore, in battle.

But Lewis, like Prince Caspian and many other fictional characters he would create over his life, emerged a victor. Despite his struggles, Lewis became known worldwide for his work on medieval literature, Christian apologetics, literary criticism, and fiction. His *Chronicles of Narnia* books alone have sold more than 100 million copies. Actor Barnes quickly signed to portray Caspian in the next installment of that series, *The Voyage of the Dawn Treader.* "[Prince Caspian is] an interesting character," says Barnes, "and I'm excited to see how he develops."

QUESTIONS
TO CONSIDER:

■ Have you read *Prince Caspian* or seen the film? What do you know about this story? Compare and contrast what you know about the life of author Lewis to his fictional prince. Can you name any other people of fact or fiction who overcame great hardship?

■ Think about a hardship you and your family have faced. How did going through that crisis strengthen you?

■ Although a time of crisis in our families may make us feel like caving in, it is possible to come through it and be stronger as a result. Today we will look at a person from biblical history who had a childhood every bit as traumatic as those of Lewis and Prince Caspian. Let's see what we can learn about emerging victorious when tough times hit our own families.

BIBLE TRUTHS

BIBLE**TRUTH** 1

Don't let difficulties defeat you. 2 KINGS 11:1-3

■ **Tell about a time when it seemed like it took all of your energy just to hang on.**

INSIDE STORY: Joash was the son of wicked King Ahaziah, who followed the pagan ways of his relatives, King Ahab and Jezebel of Israel (8:25-27). Because of his wickedness, Ahaziah was killed after spending only one year on the throne (9:14-29).

Joash was only an infant when his father died. But his problems were only beginning. His own grandmother, Athaliah, wanted to kill him and other members of the royal line so she could rule as queen! To save Joash's life, his aunt Jehosheba hid him in the temple for six years (11:1-3). But Joash endured.

Centuries later, Peter would counsel Christians, "Do not be surprised at the painful trial you are suffering, as though something strange were happening to you" (1 Peter 4:12). Suffering occurs in a world in which Satan still has influence (5:8). But we must not let a crisis defeat us.

BIBLE**TRUTH** 2

Accept increased responsibility. 2 KINGS 11:4, 19-21

■ **Has a crisis in your family ever required you to take on extra responsibilities? Tell about it.**

INSIDE STORY: In order to deal with a crisis situation, a child may have to mature quickly and assume adult responsibilities far earlier than would be normal. After six years of the tyrannical rule of Athaliah, the nation of Judah could take no more. The nation needed a king. Therefore, at the tender age of seven, Joash was revealed to be the rightful heir to the throne and assumed the rule of the kingdom of Judah (11:4, 19-21). Crisis forced Joash to accept increased responsibility at a very young age.

Sometimes God used very young people to fill important positions. When Jeremiah was called to be a prophet during the last days of the southern kingdom, Jeremiah thought himself too young for the challenge. God responded, "Do not say, 'I am only a child.' You must go to everyone I send you to and say whatever I command you" (Jeremiah 1:7). Likewise, Paul told Timothy not to let his youth stand in the way of the ministry to which he was called (1 Timothy 4:12).

BIBLE**TRUTH** 3

Find a godly role model. 2 KINGS 12:1, 2

■ **What adults in your life other than your parents have helped you mature? How have they done so?**

INSIDE STORY: How could a seven-year-old king govern? We learn that "Joash did what was right in the eyes of the LORD all the years Jehoida the priest instructed him" (12:2). A godly mentor nurtured Joash.

When crisis hits a family, often a godly adult from outside of the family must play a vital role. Hadassah was a Jewish orphan in the land of Persia. Her older cousin Mordecai assumed the role of mentor for her after the death of her parents (Esther 2:7). Through his leading, Hadassah, better known as Esther, not only survived but would also go on to save her people from extermination. Timothy's father was not a believer, so Timothy gained his faith from his mother and grandmother (Acts 16:1; 2 Timothy 1:5). The apostle Paul became a male role model for Timothy and came to refer to Timothy as "my true son in the faith" (1 Timothy 1:2).

CHALLENGE Give each student a small piece of sandpaper as a reminder of this study. Remind them that when life is rough, God can shape them the same ways that he shaped young King Joash.

THE BIG TRUTH

WHEN WE RESPECT AUTHORITY, EVERYONE BENEFITS.

CONFIDENTIAL SOURCE:
ROMANS 13:3-7

Crater with a View

Looking for an unusual gift for someone? The Lunar Embassy, a U.S. company with "authorized agents" in several other countries, may have just what you need—outer space real estate.

A few years ago, the Beijing Lunar Village Aeronautics Science and Technology Company (BLVASTC), an affiliate of the Lunar Embassy, filed suit against the government of China. For 300 yuan (about $37), a customer could buy one lunar acre and rights to all minerals up to two miles beneath its surface. Within days of the company opening for business, the Chinese government suspended the business license of BLVASTC on charges of profiteering and lunacy.

The company wanted that license back. BLVASTC claimed that its business was completely legitimate. "There is not a law or regulation in China that prohibits the selling of land on the moon," asserted chief executive officer Li Jie.

The basis of Jie's claim is a supposed loophole in the 1967 United Nations Outer Space Treaty. The treaty stipulates that no *government* can own extraterrestrial property, but does not specifically forbid *private* or *corporate* ownership. Because of this, Dennis Hope, the self-proclaimed president of the Galactic Government and "The Head Cheese" of the Lunar Embassy, filed papers with a U.S. governmental office for claim registries in San Francisco twenty-five years ago. He claimed ownership of the moon, eight planets of the solar system, and their natural satellites. He then informed the General Assembly of the United Nations and the governments of Russia and the United States. None responded, so Hope takes that as proof that his claim is valid. He followed up with a U.S. copyright registration for his company, the Lunar Embassy. "With the chaotic aspect of rules [about outer space ownership]," Hope said, "we just created our own rules."

The Lunar Embassy is a thriving worldwide business. Nearly 3.5 million lunar landowners now exist. Allegedly among them are country music stars Willie Nelson and Toby Keith, Carrie "Princess Leia" Fisher, Jerry "the Beaver" Matthers, several members of the casts of the various *Star Trek* TV shows, and Pope Benedict XVI.

QUESTIONS TO CONSIDER:

■ How seriously do you take the Lunar Embassy? Would you do business with them? Why or why not? Is it necessary for governments to get involved to regulate what it does? Explain.

■ The basic argument of the Lunar Embassy seems to be, "What we are doing is legal because no one says we *can't* do it." What do you think of that type of argument? Explain. If you were to guess, what do you think Mr. Hope believes about authority in general? What makes you think that?

■ Describe a time when you used a similar argument to rebel against authority. What happened when you, in the words of the Lunar Embassy's Dennis Hope, "just created [y]our own rules"?

■ We all have authority in our lives. Sometimes we look for loopholes rather than submitting to and showing respect to that authority. Today we'll find three biblical reasons to respect authority.

INSTANT **STUDY 32** ■ BIBLETRUTHS

BIBLE TRUTHS

BIBLE**TRUTH** 1

When we respect authority, we benefit.
ROMANS 13:3

■ **Do you have a good or bad reputation with authority figures in your life? How does your reputation affect how you are treated?**

INSIDE STORY: There are two rewards for respecting authority. When Christians obey the law, pay taxes on time, and honor the position of government leaders, they will be commended (v. 3). There may sometimes be exceptions to this principle, of course, but even dictators appreciate law-abiding citizens who don't cause trouble for them! The second reward is that others' opinions about us will improve. In the early days of Christianity, rioters claimed that Paul and his followers "caused trouble all over the world . . . saying that there is another king, one called Jesus" (Acts 17:6, 7). This was a false charge, but many espoused it. Peter urged believers to "silence the ignorant talk of foolish men" by earning a reputation for being good Roman citizens (1 Peter 2:15).

BIBLE**TRUTH** 2

When we respect authority, we escape punishment. ROMANS 13:4, 5

■ **Tell about a time when you had a guilty conscience. How did that affect you?**

INSIDE STORY: Respect also helps us avoid two negative consequences. First, those who respect authority have little to fear from the penal system! Legal authorities do "not bear the sword for nothing," Paul warned (v. 4). Such authorities are authorized to take money, freedom, and even life from criminals. But, Peter asked rhetorically, "Who is going to harm you if you are eager to do good?" (1 Peter 3:13). Secondly, failure to respect authority can result in stress brought on by a guilty conscience and fear of being caught.

But good citizens reap the reward of a good night's sleep "because of conscience" (Romans 13:5). When Paul was on trial before Roman authority but knew that he was innocent, he testified, "I strive always to keep my conscience clear before God and man" (Acts 24:16).

BIBLE**TRUTH** 3

When we respect authority, we help them do what God wants them to do. ROMANS 13:6, 7

■ **In times of crises, communities often rally together. How might that help civic leaders?**

INSIDE STORY: Finally, when we respect authority, we actually participate in stabilizing the civic order. One way is through taxation. Civil "authorities are God's servants, who give their full time to governing" (v. 6). By paying taxes we become partners with those who give their lives to promote the peace. Another way we participate is by giving respect. It is difficult to wield authority without respect. That is why Paul also wrote of the debt of honor we owe authorities (v. 7). By visibly respecting authorities we help them by encouraging others to follow our example.

CHALLENGE

Assist your students in thinking about their own lives and the amount of respect they show authority—both to God's authority and to different people in their lives. Ask them to write down a couple of authority figures they need to work on respecting. Help them come up with benefits they personally receive by showing this respect.

How can I keep my temper?

Clear and Present Anger

What makes you angry? Some situations that have caused tempers to rise have been in the news.

Sketchy Skit—The New York governor failed to laugh at a *Saturday Night Live* skit. In the skit, Governor David Paterson, who is blind, was portrayed as trying to appoint a successor to Senator Hilary Clinton. The character representing the governor held a chart upside down and described himself as being disabled and unqualified for his job. Chris Danielsen, a spokesperson for the National Federation of the Blind said the portrayal suggesting that Paterson was incompetent because of his disability is "absolutely wrong."

Fiery Friendship—Police in Indiana said a woman set fire to her ex-boyfriend's clothing at a self-storage center and caused more than $100,000 in damage. Donna J. Duell was arrested on suspicion of arson in connection with the fire. She was released from Madison County Jail after posting $20,000 bond the next day. Duell told police that she and her boyfriend were involved in a "bitter domestic dispute."

Shoe Shoo—An angry reporter made his ire known (and nearly felt) when President Bush made one of his last trips to Iraq during his presidency. As the president was addressing a crowd, the Iraqi journalist threw both of his shoes at him and shouted in Arabic, "This is your farewell kiss, you dog!" In Iraqi culture, throwing shoes at someone is a sign of contempt. Reaction in Iraq was swift but mixed, with some condemning the act and others applauding it. News stations throughout Iraq repeatedly showed footage of the incident, and newspapers carried headline stories. President Bush, who once remarked that he could look into the soul of Russian president Vladimir Putin reacted to the insult by quipping, "I didn't know what the guy said, but I saw his sole."

Basket-bite—During a heated Long Island high school basketball game, a woman put some teeth into her anger. Shaquana Beamon said that she was trying to approach her brother, a participant in the game, when a teacher pulled her to the ground and kicked her. She responded by biting the teacher's arm while someone else punched him in the head. The school district's physical education director says the teacher was working as a supervisor at the rowdy basketball game. Police say he was trying to break up the crowd.

QUESTIONS TO CONSIDER:

■ List some of the reasons for anger described in the stories above. Which reasons strike you as legitimate reasons for anger? Explain. Look at the different ways anger was expressed. What are some other ways people could have reacted?

■ What makes you angry? How do you usually deal with anger? What usually happens as a result of you dealing with your anger that way?

■ Uncontrolled anger can hurt people, damage property, and bring about other serious consequences. Let's look at the problem of uncontrolled anger and what God says about it.

BIBLE TRUTHS

BIBLE**TRUTH** 1

Prevent anger by listening more and talking less.
JAMES 1:19

■ **Tell about a time when talking too much got you into trouble.**

INSIDE STORY: "He who answers before listening—that is his folly and shame" (Proverbs 18:13). In contrast, Proverbs 12:15 tells us, "The way of a fool seems right to him, but a wise man listens to advice." Abraham Lincoln noted that God has given us all two ears and one mouth so we will listen twice as much as we speak!

When something upsets us, words seem to flow from our lips at a more rapid rate. James echoes the message of Proverbs 10:19: "When words are many, sin is not absent, but he who holds his tongue is wise."

If we don't heed James's words about listening and speaking, our anger is likely to erupt. Ignoring the prescription of active listening followed by thoughtful words can result in the equivalent of placing a burning match in a parched forest (James 3:5, 6).

BIBLE**TRUTH** 2

Prevent anger by seeking righteousness over pleasure. JAMES 1:20, 21

■ **How do you think anger is related to jealousy and selfishness?**

INSIDE STORY: Anger is fueled by our selfish desires (4:1). We must face the fact that giving in to our desires and responding in anger does not accomplish God's will (1:20).

Getting rid of something leaves a void that must be filled. God's answer is to fill it with his Word. There is no substitute for reading, studying, and reflecting upon Scripture. Regular attention to these disciplines will produce fruit, just as planting a seed in the soil eventually brings a harvest. This prescription for anger control flies in the face of the majority in our pleasure seeking culture.

What makes this counsel worth following is that it was given by Jesus himself, and it has a positive promise attached to it (Matthew 6:33). It's hard to give up something we want, but it becomes a bit easier when we realize we will get something even better in return.

BIBLE**TRUTH** 3

Prevent anger by approaching God with humility.
JAMES 1:21

■ **Do you see any correlation between arrogance and anger? Explain.**

INSIDE STORY: James expounds on verse 21 in 4:7-10. If we give in to God's authority and move toward him, he promises to draw closer to us (vv. 7, 8). In Jesus' parable of the prodigal son, when the rebellious brother came to his senses and headed for home, the father caught a glimpse of him and ran to meet him (Luke 15:20). It takes some of the edge off our anger if we realize that our concerns aren't nearly as important as God's. This brings a blessing from God (James 4:8; Psalm 24:3-5). It is also to be accompanied by repentance (James 4:9).

In contrast to God's promise to draw near to us when we step toward him, James tells us that when we stand up to Satan he will run from us (v. 7). It's similar to what we saw when Jesus was tempted in the wilderness by Satan. The devil made three tempting offers to Jesus, but to no avail. Our Lord said no and responded by speaking words of Scripture to his accuser. Satan tucked his tail between his legs and ran. When Satan fled, God sent angels to take his place and minister to Jesus (Matthew 4:1-11).

CHALLENGE

Gather in a circle and ask students to think of a situation that tempts them toward uncontrolled anger. One at a time, allow them to confess the situation that causes them to lose control of their anger.

Is it OK to be angry sometimes?

Suppressing Dissent

The First Amendment of the U.S. Constitution allows American citizens to express their displeasure with those who hold power. But not every nation allows freedom of speech and freedom of the press. What happens when a government tries to "bottle up" the anger of its citizens?

One answer can be seen in past events in China. A few years ago, three editors of the *Beijing News* were fired. Analysts believed the dismissals showed that the Communist Party remained determined to maintain control over the media. "In China you need to know how to do things, and there are boundaries that you are not supposed to overstep," said Lu Yiyi, a researcher at an international affairs institute in London.

The following day, about one hundred journalists—one third of the *Beijing News* staff—went out on strike. The *Beijing News* was published on Friday but the names of its editors, normally printed on the paper's masthead, had been omitted.

The firings and ensuing strike seemed to be the results of the newspaper's criticism of the government. The paper reported the violent suppression of rioting farmers and fishermen in Dongzhou, China by armed police. The editors also exposed official corruption and poor government decision making.

The New York-based "Committee to Protect Journalists" claimed that China punishes more journalists than any other government. On another occasion, Zhao Yan, a Chinese researcher for *The New York Times*, was charged with disclosing state secrets. A little later, the deputy editor of the *Southern Metropolitan News* was fired for reporting that a government official was found to be responsible for a fatal coalmine accident. Shi Tao, a former editor of *Contemporary*

Business News in Hunan Province, is serving a ten-year sentence in a high security prison for distributing on the Internet what a court ruled were state secrets. Also, a reporter for Singapore's *Straits Times* was tried for espionage after his arrest in southern China.

Despite the crackdown, many Chinese journalists believe that social and economic change in China as well as changes in technology will make it very difficult for the authorities to keep reporters from expressing the anger of Chinese citizens. They pledge to continue reporting news that the Chinese government might find to be unfavorable.

QUESTIONS TO CONSIDER:

■ How often do you read a newspaper, review news on the Internet, or watch TV news broadcasts? How might you react if you felt that the government was "bottling up" public anger against national policies by refusing to allow that anger to be expressed? Consider the situation in China. What is your opinion of this newspaper strike? Why do you believe some journalists might go along with government demands and not print negative news?

■ Have you ever tried to keep yourself from expressing anger, fearing that you would get in trouble if you did so? Explain. Were you able to suppress your anger for long? Why or why not?

■ Not allowing anger to be expressed can be as devastating as anger that is out of control. Healthy anger can bring about positive changes in personal relationships as well as in society at large. Let's look at what the Bible says about expressing anger in a healthy manner.

INSTANT **STUDY 34** ■ BIBLE**TRUTHS**

BIBLE TRUTHS

BIBLE**TRUTH** 1

Healthy anger is rooted in truth, not falsehood.
EPHESIANS 4:25

■ **Have you ever said, "I don't want to talk about it," when you were angry? Why might that be a bad idea?**

INSIDE STORY: First, we must "put off falsehood" (v. 25). We tend to think we are rarely, if ever, at fault. Personal attacks may trigger an aggressive defense reaction because we cling to a false perception. Healthy anger recognizes the truth of our own sinfulness (Romans 3:23). Anger can be made productive when we consider an insult and ask, "What can I learn about myself because of what was said to me?"

In contrast, Jesus' anger was caused when people who should have known better were flagrantly disobeying God's truth and harming others in the process (Matthew 21:12, 13; 23).

In Psalm 15:2, David identifies a person who "speaks the truth from his heart" as one who will live in the presence of God. Truth is such a critical issue in the life of the believer that Jesus even identified himself as "the truth" (John 14:6). Satan, to the contrary, is identified as a liar and the father of lies (8:44).

BIBLE**TRUTH** 2

Healthy anger seeks resolution, not dominance.
EPHESIANS 4:26, 27

■ **Tell of someone you know who just loves to argue. Do you think he or she really wants to resolve a problem? Why or why not?**

INSIDE STORY: Both Paul and Jesus commanded us to make reconciliation a high priority, especially with others who follow Jesus. Even if we are right in the middle of worshiping God, Jesus instructs us to interrupt it, meet with our brother, and then return to worship (Matthew 5:23, 24). This is in perfect harmony with Paul's admonition to not end the day while still angry (Ephesians 4:26). Anger that is allowed to sit, soak, and settle is a problem in the making.

Jesus instructs us to "settle matters quickly,"(Matthew 5:25). It can be damaging to hold onto anger and simmer and stew over a period of time. Jesus makes it clear that a failure to deal with anger in a timely manner can allow it to escalate to dangerous proportions. The goal is to resolve a problem, not to win an argument.

The devil's name, Satan, is really a title. It is the Hebrew word for *adversary*. When we let a problem with another believer go unresolved, we are casting a child of God in the adversarial role reserved for Satan. No wonder Paul calls this giving "the devil a foothold" (Ephesians 4:27)! Unresolved conflict separates Christians.

BIBLE**TRUTH** 3

Healthy anger is used to bring positive results.
EPHESIANS 4:28

■ **Tell of a time when a relationship was strengthened by resolving a problem.**

INSIDE STORY: Wrong behavior must cease, and right behavior must begin. Hands that have been taking from others must put an end to these actions and are now instructed to work in order to create something that can be shared with others. Anger that has stolen joy, peace, and health can actually be used to replace it and rebuild it.

Expressing anger appropriately has been something people have continually struggled with. Aristotle summed it up when he said, "Anyone can become angry, but to be angry with the right person, to the right degree, at the right time, for the right purpose, and in the right way—this is not easy."

CHALLENGE

Distribute small notebooks and encourage students to keep anger journals. In these journals they should record when and how they reacted in anger. Reviewing them privately, they may find better ways of expressing anger.

CONFIDENTIAL SOURCE:
MATTHEW 18:15-20

THE CHURCH HAS ALWAYS BEEN IN THE
CONFLICT RESOLUTION BUSINESS.

How can I heal a broken relationship?

Bitter Battles

Some people handle conflict better than others. But some people get way out of control. Read the following unhealthy ways people have dealt with recent conflict:

A penny for your thoughts—A Canadian man was angered when he discovered that the company he had a credit card with was having some of its processing work done in the United States. Don Rogers thought that the U.S. government would then have access to his credit card records. To retaliate, Rogers went online and began paying his bill one penny at a time. Because he placed so many small online transactions per day, the credit card company's computers jammed. One report said that an attempt to print Rogers's billing statement ended up with a printout over thirty-two feet long.

A cold reaction—Johnny Joe Mercado from Minnesota was driving down the road on a snowy day when his car was pelted with a snowball by some teens looking for a laugh. But the boys weren't laughing when Mercado turned around and followed them home. There, Mercado allegedly punched and kicked the thirteen-year-old and demanded that the fifteen-year-old take off a gold earring and necklace he was wearing and hand it over. The boys said Mercado also threatened to kill them if they called the police. But the boys did tell authorities about the crime and Mercado was arrested for a felony charge of robbery and a misdemeanor charge of assault.

A hot temper—In 2004, a South Korean man was charged a $300 fine for disturbing the peace. He had caused a ruckus at a cell phone store when he didn't like the phone number he had been given. The man appealed his sentence. So some months later, he was in court again. When the judge agreed that he indeed had to pay the fine, the man reacted in anger by storming out of the courtroom and pouring heating oil on himself. He then walked back into the courtroom and set himself on fire. He was taken to the hospital, suffering from third-degree burns.

QUESTIONS TO CONSIDER:

■ Which reaction to conflict seems the most outrageous to you? If you were one of the three men in the articles, which situation would make you the most angry? What would you have done differently to handle such conflict?

■ How do you usually react when conflict happens? Name some of the worst ways you've ever handled conflict.

■ Unfortunately, life will always involve different types of conflicts. Since we can't avoid conflict, we need a plan for handling it. Let's look at a biblical method for handling conflict.

BIBLE TRUTHS

BIBLE**TRUTH** 1

Attempt to resolve conflict with a private, face-to-face confrontation. MATTHEW 18:15

■ **Tell about a time when a friend pointed out that you had a smudge on your face or that you had a button off of your shirt. How did you respond? Would you have responded differently if a friend was correcting your behavior rather than your appearance? Why?**

INSIDE STORY: Jesus refused to label his followers as the important and the unimportant. Even the "little ones" must not be allowed to perish (18:6). Even one stray sheep must be diligently sought (v. 12). Likewise, a renegade brother must not just be written off. Jesus outlined a specific situation dealing with a close friend or relative, a "brother" (v. 15). The goal of biblical conflict resolution is not winning an argument but preserving a relationship. God wants Christians to be bound together in friendship in this world and also in the next (v. 18).

Minor annoyances that are not sin are best simply forgotten (Proverbs 12:16). But when the problem involves an offense that Scripture calls sin, it should not be swept under the carpet (Matthew 18:15). The person who has been offended is told to confront the sinning brother. This is to be done privately and gently, not with arrogance or self-righteousness (Galatians 6:1). Sometimes this is enough to solve the problem.

BIBLE**TRUTH** 2

Use reliable witnesses, if necessary, to support your position. MATTHEW 18:16

■ **List some Internet rumors you have heard. What would it take to convince you that one of them was true?**

INSIDE STORY: Sometimes the accused may grow angry, cast blame, or outright deny the allegation. In that case, the injured party is to take one or two others along to be witnesses (v. 16). The concept of having two or three

witnesses against someone accused of wrongdoing is a key element of Old Testament law (Deuteronomy 19:15). Before making an accusation against another, we must rely on eyewitness accounts, not gossip or hearsay. If two or three witnesses are willing to gather and testify to the truth of what they saw, we can make sure that Christ is with us in our search for reconciliation (Matthew 18:19, 20). Often, this intervention of friends is enough to reconcile the estranged parties.

BIBLE**TRUTH** 3

Publicly separate yourself from the offending party if you are unable to resolve the matter. MATTHEW 18:17

■ **It has been said, "Be careful what you wish for; you may get it." When was that true in your life?**

INSIDE STORY: But problems may persist. If the offending party still won't listen, the matter must be told to the whole church (v. 17). At this point the offender is reminded that his wrongdoing is more than an offense against one person. It has to do with calling him back into an honest relationship with God. Therefore, refusal to reconcile is a refusal to be associated with other believers. Therefore, he is to be treated like the outsider he has chosen to be (1 Corinthians 5:10-13; 2 Thessalonians 3:14). It is hard to back away from a relationship, but there may come a time when we must recognize that someone values his or her sin over our friendship. Continuing a dysfunctional relationship at that point helps no one.

CHALLENGE

Hand out short lengths of rope tied into a knot. Remind students of the need to keep the bond with other Christians strong with this acrostic:

Keep praying for my Christian brother or sister.

Nurture my Christian brother or sister to a deeper faith.

Overlook irritating faults of my Christian brother or sister.

Trust my Christian brother or sister who has once hurt me.

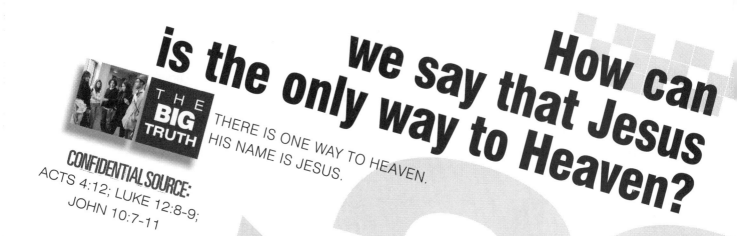

How can we say that Jesus is the only way to Heaven?

THE BIG TRUTH

THERE IS ONE WAY TO HEAVEN. HIS NAME IS JESUS.

CONFIDENTIAL SOURCE:
ACTS 4:12; LUKE 12:8-9;
JOHN 10:7-11

Academic Shortcut

All across the country, school districts want to increase the percentage of students who graduate from high school. But how can that happen when students fail to pass required courses? A growing answer for many is a shortcut to graduation called *credit recovery*.

Credit recovery can mean different things for different schools. The Cyber Oregon Online (COOL) School program is the electronic alternative school program for that northwestern state. "A credit recovery course," according to the COOL School Web site, "is a shortened version of a regular education course. It teaches the same concepts, but it is limited in the amount of practice activities and student-to-student interaction."

The Greeley-Evans School District 6 in Colorado offers credit recovery classes after school, at night, and via the Internet to help students make up their missing credits. Maria Hope Gomez believes her two sons benefited from credit recovery. At one point, one of her sons was failing five high school classes. "The programs allowed them to make up the work," Gomez said. "I appreciate the fact they had the chance to make up the credit."

Not everyone is a fan of credit recovery, however. In New York City, many teachers call credit recovery programs a poor substitute for classroom learning. When Dennis Bunyan failed his first-semester senior English class in that city, he was allowed to earn the credit he needed for graduation by writing three essays. His English teacher,

Charan Morris, was so troubled that she boycotted Bunyan's graduation ceremony. Morris wrote that she believed some students were "being pushed through the system regardless of whether they have done the work to earn their diploma."

What does Bunyan have to say about being allowed to take this shortcut? "I'm grateful for it, but it also just seems kind of, you know, outrageous," the student said. "There's no way three essays can possibly cover a semester of work."

QUESTIONS TO CONSIDER:

■ Is there a credit recovery program in your school district? What is required for credit recovery? Do you believe this shortcut is fair? Why or why not?

■ What are some popular shortcuts that you have heard about? (e.g., a quick way to get a job done, a quick way to get healthy, a quick way to get rich)

■ What "quick fixes" or shortcuts have you been tempted to try? How did they work for you?

■ People disagree as to whether or not it is fair to use credit recovery as a shortcut to avoid taking a full class. After all, we all like to take shortcuts sometimes. Some would even like to believe that there are shortcuts to God. These might include meditation, rituals, or good works. But the Bible tells us that there is no shortcut. Let's look at why Jesus said that he is the only way to Heaven.

BIBLE TRUTHS

BIBLE**TRUTH** 1

Only Jesus unleashes God's power. ACTS 4:12

■ **Years ago barbers also acted as surgeons. Would you go to a barber today if you needed your appendix removed? Why is that *not* a "narrow view" of barbering?**

INSIDE STORY: All of the people watching him in the area of the temple called Solomon's Colonnade were amazed. They knew that he had been horribly crippled since birth, and he had been begging every day by the gate of the temple for as long as they could remember. But there he was, healed completely in the name of Jesus Christ (3:6, 7). The disturbance in the temple came to the attention of the temple guard and the Sadducees who were responsible for temple affairs. The next day, the religious leaders of Jerusalem assembled and demanded of Peter and John, "By what power or what name did you do this?" (4:7). Peter replied boldly, "It is by the name of Jesus Christ of Nazareth, whom you crucified but whom God raised from the dead, that this man stands before you healed" (v. 10). Further, Peter said, "Salvation is found in no one else, for there is no other name under heaven given to men by which we must be saved" (v. 12).

We live in a time when it is popular to discount the exclusive claims of Jesus. Yet, we can believe that Jesus is the only way to God after seeing God's power unleashed in his name alone.

BIBLE**TRUTH** 2

Only Jesus pleads our case in Heaven. LUKE 12:8, 9

■ **Whom do you know who has been represented by an attorney? List some reasons people need lawyers.**

INSIDE STORY: Jesus was in Judea, the province that held Jerusalem, the center of religious and political power. Jesus began warning of the hypocrisy of the religious establishment. The Pharisees would not look to the best interests of the people and would betray them if the need arose (12:1-3). Jesus immediately followed by telling the crowds that those

devoted to God had nothing to fear from "those who kill the body," the occupying Roman forces (vv. 4-7). At that point, Jesus called for allegiance to himself. Religious or political leaders could not do what the Son of Man could do. Jesus was the only one who could represent the interests of human beings in the courts of Heaven (vv. 8, 9)! Only Jesus "speaks to the Father in our defense" (1 John 2:1).

BIBLE**TRUTH** 3

Only Jesus gave his life for ours. JOHN 10:7-11

■ **Imagine that someone who was not your friend gave you an organ transplant that saved your life. How might your relationship with that person change?**

INSIDE STORY: Jesus often illustrated his teaching with allusions to the relationship of shepherds and sheep. A flock will follow a shepherd through the crowded streets of a town and recognize the voice of their shepherd. Jesus used this to illustrate his special role of leadership, protection, and love for his followers.

Often sheep would be gathered in a sheep pen for protection at night. Jesus spoke of himself as the gate to that place of protection, saying, "I am the gate; whoever enters through me will be saved" (v. 9). In contrast to thieves who come to steal and kill the sheep, he has come to bring life to them—abundant and full life. In fact, he lays down his life for the sheep. Our good shepherd has the right to insist that we hear only his voice, because only he gave his life to save ours.

CHALLENGE Have students pray, confessing to God some ways they have looked for shortcuts to him.

How does Islam differ from Christianity?

THE BIG TRUTH

CONFIDENTIAL SOURCE:
MATTHEW 12:1, 2, 7, 8;
JOHN 4:21;
1 PETER 2:21-23

BIBLICAL CHRISTIANITY AND ISLAM DISAGREE ABOUT HOW A PERSON GETS RIGHT WITH GOD.

Silly Success

Most of us are familiar with Nobel Prizes. These prestigious awards honor those who have made great achievements in fields such as chemistry, physics, medicine, economics, literature, and contributing to world peace. The Nobel Prizes are awarded every December. But two months before, the *Ig Nobel* Prizes poke fun at scientists who have sought success by performing far less significant research.

The Ig Nobel Prizes are a parody of the Nobel Prizes and are given for ten achievements that "first make people laugh, and then make them think." Organized by the scientific humor magazine *Annals of Improbable Research (AIR),* they are presented by a group that includes some genuine Nobel Laureates at a ceremony at Harvard University's Sanders Theater. (Actor Russell Johnson, known for his portrayal of the Professor on the TV series *Gilligan's Island,* once participated in the award presentation ceremony as "The Professor Emeritus of Gilligan's Island"!)

Here are some Ig Nobel Prize recipients for the year 2008:

The Ig Nobel Prize for Nutrition—Massimiliano Zampini of the University of Trento, Italy, and Charles Spence of Britain's Oxford University tricked people into thinking they were eating fresh potato chips by playing loud, crunching sounds when people bit one.

The Ig Nobel Prize for Physics—Dorian Raymer of the Scripps Institution in San Diego and a colleague demonstrated mathematically why hair or a ball of string will inevitably tangle itself in knots.

The Ig Nobel Prize for Biology—A hard-working team of French zoologists made the profound discovery that dog fleas can jump higher than cat fleas.

The Ig Nobel Peace Prize—The Swiss Federal Ethics Committee on Non-Human Biotechnology adopted the legal principle that plants, like animals, "should also be protected from unjustified interventions on their appearance [and] from humiliation."

Each Ig Nobel Prize ceremony is traditionally closed with the words, "If you didn't win a prize—and especially if you did—better luck next year!"

QUESTIONS TO CONSIDER:

■ Why do you find the scientific findings of these prizewinners funny? Why might you also find it sad that people would spend time and money trying to seek success with these projects?

■ What are some other ways people seek success? Why might some of those quests for success seem foolish to some?

■ But how should we seek success? What achievements really matter in the long term? Today, let's look at what defines success in the eyes of God—and how that view differs from the view of other religions.

BIBLE**TRUTH** 1

We are to follow the example of Jesus who came to serve, not conquer. 1 PETER 2:21-23

■ **Our society teaches that we should look out for Number One. What evidence of that have you seen?**

INSIDE STORY: Some say that to be successful in this difficult world one must be aggressive. Christians, however, are to follow the example of a suffering Savior. Jesus submitted himself to his enemies, trusting in a just God (vv. 21-23). Christians are to "turn the other cheek" when confronted with evil, not buy a bigger gun (Matthew 5:39-41). Just as Jesus was glorified by giving his life, those who would follow him must be willing to give up life in order to gain it (John 12:23-26; Luke 9:24-26). Success does not come by being a warrior in a physical battle, but by being "as sheep to be slaughtered" (Romans 8:32, 33, 36, 37).

Islam stands in direct contrast with Christianity in this way. Radical Muslims declare that jihad is necessary to physically destroy the enemies of God and to bring justice. Most Muslims do not accept this radical view, but they still reject "turning the other cheek."

BIBLE**TRUTH** 2

We get close to God by developing a relationship with him, not through rituals. MATTHEW 12:1, 2, 7, 8

■ **Imagine that you had a friend who spoke the exact same words to you in every conversation. How deep would your friendship be?**

INSIDE STORY: Jesus ridiculed the ritualistic view of giving, prayer, fasting, and Sabbath keeping that was popular in his day (6:2, 7, 16; 12:1, 2). Rather, Jesus said that one does not build a relationship with God through ritual, but by sharing God's goals of mercy and reconciliation (12:7, 8; Hosea 6:6). Micah taught that God did not want ritual, but desired that his people show their love by modeling his character (Micah 6:6-8).

Unlike Christianity, Islam focuses upon ritual. Five times each day Muslims rise, cleanse with water, and present themselves directly before Allah in *salat*, ritual prayer. Every Muslim whose financial condition is above a certain specified minimum must pay at least 2.5 percent of his savings annually in the ritual of *zakat*, almsgiving. During the ninth month of the lunar year, Muslims practice *sawm*, fasting during daylight hours, breaking their fasts after dusk.

BIBLE**TRUTH** 3

No one geographical area is more holy than any other. JOHN 4:21

■ **Say you do not phone or text your friends, but will only speak to them when you see them. What might they think about that?**

INSIDE STORY: When speaking to a woman of Samaria, Jesus said that in his kingdom, God would be worshiped anywhere by those who were truly his (vv. 21, 24). Paul chided the people of Athens, telling them that the true God does not live in such temples (Acts 17:24). Paul knew what Jeremiah had preached centuries before, that Jehovah was not "only a God nearby," but also "a God far away" (Jeremiah 23:23). Pleasing God is not a matter of geography.

Geography is *very* important in Islam, however. Islam teaches that Abraham and Ishmael built the first temple in Mecca, Saudi Arabia. Therefore, it is important for Muslims to face that holy spot when they pray. It is also required that any Muslim financially able to do so must physically travel to Mecca once in his or her lifetime.

CHALLENGE Provide some resources about Islam and how it differs from Christianity to your group.

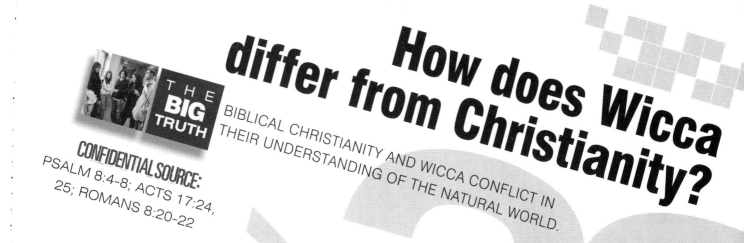

How does Wicca differ from Christianity?

THE BIG TRUTH

BIBLICAL CHRISTIANITY AND WICCA CONFLICT IN THEIR UNDERSTANDING OF THE NATURAL WORLD.

CONFIDENTIAL SOURCE:
PSALM 8:4-8; ACTS 17:24, 25; ROMANS 8:20-22

Nature's Fury

It is hard not to be awed by the breathtaking beauty of the Kashmir Valley. The magnificent Himalayan Mountains almost appear to cradle this land of northern Pakistan in a safe embrace. But on Saturday, October 8, 2008, any illusion of security was shattered. A violent earthquake, measuring 7.6 on the Richter scale, obliterated villages and killed tens of thousands of people. The quake was the worst natural disaster to hit Pakistan since its formation in 1947 and one of the most destructive earthquakes in the world in the past one hundred years.

Tariq Farooq, the communication minister in Kashmir reported, "More than 30,000 people have died in the earthquake in Kashmir. . . . There are cities, there are towns which have been completely destroyed." Farooq estimated that more than 60 percent of houses, shops, and buildings in Muzaffarabad had been obliterated. "Bodies are scattered in the city," said Masood-ur Rehman, the assistant commissioner of Muzaffarabad. "We are helpless."

Pakistani president Prevez Musharraf said the earthquake was a testing time for the country and expressed the belief that the nation would come up to the challenge. "It is a challenging time for the nation and I urge the people to face this calamity with courage," he said. "We are doing whatever is humanly possible," promised Musharraf. "We are trying to reach all those areas where people need our help."

Most earthquakes are caused by shifting in the earth's crust. Although the earth seems solid and stable, it is actually made up of large plates that slide over a layer of liquid rock under them. In this case, the Indian plate on which the country of India is located was pressing against the Eurasian plate on which most of Pakistan is located. The two countries literally crashed into one another several miles below the surface.

Over the past half-century, India and Pakistan have fought two wars over Kashmir and came close to engaging in a third. This led the reader of an Indian newspaper to merge science, politics, and philosophy and comment, "The fundamentalist elements [of Pakistan and India] have been trying desperately to create distances between the two countries often by killing innocent people. . . . However, nature wills otherwise. Nature is pushing India closer and closer to Pakistan. . . . Perhaps this is nature's way of asking people to come closer or else . . ."

QUESTIONS
TO CONSIDER:

■ Have you or anyone else you know ever been in an earthquake? Describe the feelings involved in such an experience.

■ The world is full of natural wonders. Tell about some you have seen or would like to visit. How does hearing of a natural disaster affect your view of natural beauty? How does it make you feel to know that something very beautiful can change quickly into something incredibly dangerous?

■ Consider the quote at the end of the article, especially how the writer gives human characteristics (such as intelligence and will) to nature. What do you think of that philosophy?

■ The natural world is certainly beautiful. But some religions and philosophies almost worship nature. The Bible has a different view. Let's discover what the Bible says about our world and contrast it with a popular, nature-centered religion.

INSTANT **STUDY 38** ■ **BIBLETRUTHS**

BIBLE**TRUTH** 1

God exists apart from nature. ACTS 17:24, 25

■ **Remember *Star Wars*? How is the Force described in those films different from what you know about God?**

INSIDE STORY: God is *everywhere*, but he is separate from *everything*. God thinks and acts differently than even the most gifted human being (Isaiah 55:8). In fact, pagan religions are foolish attempts to deny God and to pretend human beings can actually be of aid to him (Romans 1:22, 23; Acts 17:24, 25). God is spirit, and his creatures must acknowledge this truth (John 4:24).

Furthermore, God is eternal, "from everlasting to everlasting," while the natural world is created by him and is temporary (Psalm 90:2). Even human beings, though glorious creatures, have a fixed lifespan and "return to dust" (vv. 3, 10). God is not a disembodied life force that emanates from nature. He is the intelligent, eternal creator of nature.

Wicca, modern witchcraft, is ancient paganism in contemporary clothing. Wicca teaches that every living organism has a spirit, and that those spirits are connected. This giant, spiritual web of nature, they believe, is God—an impersonal, unknowable life force.

BIBLE**TRUTH** 2

Human beings are unique in God's natural creation. PSALM 8:4-8

■ **A friend tells you that she believes that human beings are "potential gods." How might you respond?**

INSIDE STORY: God empowered human beings to care for and rule the natural world (vv. 6-8; Genesis 1:26). Of utmost importance, human beings are different from animals because they alone are created in God's image (v. 27). But humans are still creatures, not potential gods. We were created to share characteristics of God—personality, creativity, morality, self-determination, etc.—but we were created "a little lower than the heavenly beings" (Psalm 8:5). Humans are neither highly evolved animals nor potential deities.

Wicca also differs from this biblical teaching. According to modern witchcraft, human beings are not subject to God's law but are capable of determining right and wrong on their own. Wicca says human beings derive authority from being properly aligned with nature.

BIBLE**TRUTH** 3

Nature has been corrupted by sin. ROMANS 8:20-22

■ **Some say that they can be closer to God by communing with nature than by being in church. What do you say?**

INSIDE STORY: The Bible teaches that at the end of creation, the natural world was wholly good (Genesis 1:31). But then the first man and woman rebelled against God's authority (3:17). The resulting catastrophe affected the entire natural world. Weeds grew up to inhibit the growth of edible plants (vv. 18, 19). Until the time when the first world will be destroyed and replaced, nature is figuratively groaning in pain (Revelation 21:1; Romans 8:20-22).

We can learn quite a lot about God's power and nature by observing nature (Psalm 19:1; Romans 1:20). But natural revelation is incomplete in and of itself. We also need a special revelation from God's Word to have a complete knowledge of God (Psalm 19:7-11).

Wicca disagrees. Wiccans believe that special revelation is unnecessary and that nature alone teaches all truth. Furthermore, Wicca teaches that sin and salvation are outdated concepts. They say that what we call evil is just a necessary aspect of good.

CHALLENGE

Provide some resources about Wicca and how it differs from Christianity to your group.

THE BIG TRUTH

LET US EXPLORE CYBERSPACE WISELY.

CONFIDENTIAL SOURCE:
PROVERBS 1:10, 11, 18, 19;
MATTHEW 10:26, 27;
EPHESIANS 5:15, 16

Should I use the Internet?

Armed and Dangerous

Some argue that guns are good. Others argue that guns are bad. Check out these stories.

Saving Private Gump—Actor Tom Hanks angered some gun control advocates by hiring an armed security guard to patrol one of his homes. The actor was in the process of suing the builders of the home for shoddy construction. While Hanks admitted that the contractor he was taking to court had the right to look for evidence to defend himself, the actor did not want the contractor and his representatives to enter his property unannounced and to be on his property unsupervised.

Opposing lawyers said that the armed guard posed a threat to anyone on Hanks's land. Attorney Miles Stanislaw complained, "The other day, the guard tripped and fell on a piece of plywood with his gun on him. It could have gone off and had fatal consequences." The security guard himself, Shane Gilbert, took exception to that remark. "I'm very well-trained and capable," said Gilbert. "Security guards don't pack heat just to go around shooting people."

Attacking the Lawn Boy—Keith Walendowski's lawnmower wouldn't start. So the fifty-six-year-old Milwaukee man shot it with a short-barreled shotgun. Walendowski was charged with felony possession of a firearm and misdemeanor disorderly conduct while armed.

Walendowski faced up to an $11,000 fine and six years and three months in prison if convicted. Authorities have said that alcohol consumption may have been a contributing factor in the incident.

Missing the Mark—A Florida couple spotted an animal in their yard and went outside to investigate. The intruder turned out to be a fox. The animal attacked the woman, biting her left leg and refusing to let go.

At his wife's request the man got his .22-caliber rifle to shoot the fox. After firing seven shots, the man killed the animal, but also hit his wife in the right leg. The fox was sent to a lab to be tested for rabies and the woman was sent to a nearby hospital for treatment.

QUESTIONS
TO CONSIDER:

■ Take a look at each story above. In what ways were firearms used and misused? Explain how using a gun can have either positive or negative consequences. What are some factors that make the difference?

■ Name some other things that can be used with either positive or negative results. For example, a cell phone can bring help when someone is in a car accident. But it can also *cause* an accident if a person is driving while using it.

■ There are many things that are not good or evil in themselves but that can have good or bad consequences depending on how they are used. The Internet can certainly be beneficial if used in certain ways. Yet it can be harmful if used in other ways. Today we'll look at some biblical principles for using the Internet wisely and safely.

BIBLE TRUTHS

BIBLE**TRUTH** 1

Monitor the amount of time you spend online.
EPHESIANS 5:15, 16

■ **Tell about a situation in which it is easy for you to lose track of time.**

INSIDE STORY: Paul warned the Ephesians that they should be "redeeming the time" (Ephesians 5:16, *KJV*). Human beings have limited time on this planet that quickly passes. Therefore we must "number our days aright," guarding our time conscientiously and investing it wisely (Psalm 90:12). We are not guaranteed another day to live, but we are responsible for the hours in every day that we are granted.

One of the symptoms of Internet addiction is time distortion. It is very easy to lose track of time when online. The biblical advice to treat time as a precious commodity should be heeded by those who surf the Web.

BIBLE**TRUTH** 2

Keep yourself from physical and spiritual danger.
PROVERBS 1:10, 11, 18, 19

■ **List some dangers of the Internet. How easy is it to avoid those dangers?**

INSIDE STORY: Solomon spoke often of the value of hanging with the right crowd (vv. 10, 11). As Paul would warn followers of Jesus centuries later, "Bad company corrupts good character" (1 Corinthians 15:33). The problem is that those who are in the company of the wrong crowd eventually share their fate. While they seek to victimize others, "they only waylay themselves" (Proverbs 1:18). "A man reaps what he sows" (Galatians 6:7).

While the Internet has much to offer, it can be a dangerous place. The anonymity that it can offer makes it a fertile field for temptation. Accountability to other Christians, friends, and family members is wise. Even the simple act of keeping a door open when online helps dampen the fires of temptation and danger.

BIBLE**TRUTH** 3

Use the Internet as a tool for sharing your faith.
MATTHEW 10:26, 27

■ **Do you have a MySpace or Facebook page? How do you use it?**

INSIDE STORY: When Jesus was about to send out his disciples, he gave them advice for spreading his teachings. Jesus encouraged them to take his message and "proclaim [it] from the roofs" (v. 27). A gathering of friends on a rooftop was a time of effective teaching. This is essentially what Peter encouraged Christians to do years later when he wrote, "Always be prepared to give an answer to everyone who asks you to give the reason for the hope that you have" (1 Peter 3:15). Disciples of Christ look for opportunities to share their faith.

The Internet is a modern-day "rooftop." People from all over the world gather daily to converse with others. The opportunities to have casual conversations about those things that truly matter abound for Christians of all ages. Many companies offer the opportunity for anyone to begin an online discussion group. Yahoo!, for example, has over 10,000 groups dedicated to the discussion of Christianity. Nearly 3,000 of those groups are teen or student groups. Blogs (short for Web logs) are similar forums. A blogger creates a site (usually at no charge) with personal journal entries on a topic of his or her choosing. Viewers are invited to respond. Thousands of blogs are dedicated to discussion of Christianity, with the number growing daily.

CHALLENGE

Lead your group in this visualized prayer: Close your eyes and imagine that you are on your computer. All of a sudden you receive an IM from Jesus! He writes, "How much time have U spent online 2day?" Respond. Then he asks, "Do your parents know what UR doing online?" Respond. Finally he says, "How do people online know U belong 2 me?" Respond. Now imagine yourself typing back a response in which you promise to alter your online conduct. What do you say?

THE BIG TRUTH

CONFIDENTIAL SOURCE:
PSALM 1:1-3; 137:7-9;
SONG OF SONGS 4:1-3

MUSIC IS A GIFT OF GOD THAT CAN REACH INTO OUR EMOTIONAL DEPTHS.

Does God approve of my music?

Expressing the Inexpressible

Have you ever experienced so many emotions that words could not express how you felt? There are many outlets for emotions, but oftentimes people find that creating in art forms can help express their feelings.

Rays of Hope Children's Grief Center in Midland, Texas, recognizes the need for children to voice their emotions as they deal with death, divorce, or separation anxiety. To that end, the center sponsors M.A.D. (Music, Art, and Drama) Camp. This program helps kids ages five to eighteen express their grief by using a variety of art forms.

"Kids have a need to do the work of grieving, and we need to give them permission and tools of expression so they can do that work," said Vicki Jay, director of Rays of Hope. "We focus on using their natural tools like music, art, and drama to do the work of the heart—those feelings inside—by finding appropriate ways to express those feelings," she continued.

Eleven-year-old Elizabeth Wollaston said the M.A.D. camp helped her figure out her feelings about her parents' divorce and the loss of a loved one. "It's OK to express yourself here," she said.

Across the ocean, continents away from Texas, sits Muneer Awwad, a twenty-one-year-old Palestinian living in Israel. His life has been filled with the emotions that war and conflict bring. At age five, he experienced tear gas being thrown into his home. Years later at age seventeen, his cousin died from tear gas. Muneer was overwhelmed by his cousin's death. To deal with it, he went home and wrote rap music. "The second the ink left the pen and got caught on the paper, all the stress, all the problems, the hopes, the dreams got trapped on the paper. Writing rhymes was my therapy," Muneer said.

Rap began in urban America, but it has since spanned the globe, becoming a voice for young people to write about the pain experienced in conflict and war. Although the form of rap is fairly new, creating to express emotion during war is not a new concept. During the Civil War, songs such as "When Johnny Comes Marching Home" were written. In World War I, soldiers wrote poetry such as "In Flanders Field" to express the horrors they saw.

Although the forms of creativity may change, the therapy of creating will continue as people find ways to explain the emotions churning inside them.

QUESTIONS TO CONSIDER:

■ Name a situation in which you had trouble expressing your emotions. How did you end up sharing your feelings? Does creating help you express emotion? If so, what forms of creating help you? If not, what things do you do to express your feelings?

■ We express our emotions in a variety of ways. Just like the people discussed in the article, one way we can express our feelings is through music. Let's look at the ways people in the Bible also used music to express themselves.

BIBLE**TRUTH** 1

Music can communicate the core values of a group of people. PSALM 1:1-3

■ **Tell about a time when you said, "That song expresses exactly how I feel."**

INSIDE STORY: Psalms was the songbook of the Jews and early Christians. Psalm 1 promises that those who reject the standards of the world and embrace the commands of God are nourished and strengthened (vv. 2, 3). Christians in the first century encouraged other believers to be true to their core values (Hebrews 10:23). This often happened in corporate worship (vv. 24, 25). Part of this worship included singing psalms (Colossians 3:16). The words of many Psalms are still regularly sung in times of worship (8:1, 2; 9:1, 2; 118:1, 24).

The words of Psalm 1 became the basis for the spiritual, "I Shall Not Be Moved." This song has been sung in worship and was a theme song of the civil rights movement in the mid-twentieth century. Patriotic songs, such as "America the Beautiful" and "God Bless America," serve the purpose of uniting the singers in a bond of shared beliefs and loyalties. Rock anthems such as The Who's "My Generation" and P.O.D.'s "Youth of the Nation" serve a similar purpose. Music can be used to draw like-minded people together.

BIBLE**TRUTH** 2

Music can express anger and frustration.
PSALM 137:7-9

■ **Some songs have angry lyrics. List some of them. Does that make them bad? Defend your answer.**

INSIDE STORY: Not all Psalms were joyful praise songs. Psalm 137 expresses the anger of a war-scarred people who dreamt of unspeakable vengeance. But the Bible always separates anger and acting upon that anger in a sinful manner (4:4). We must "Hate evil, [and] love good" (Amos 5:15). Yet songs are a legitimate way of expressing

righteous anger. David regularly sang of his hope for the humiliation of his enemies (Psalm 109:6-15). Job bitterly complained that God seemed slow to punish evildoers (Job 24:1-4). The prophets sang with a nearly bloodthirsty glee about the defeat of their enemies (Obadiah 6-9; Nahum 3:1-4).

The use of music to express anger is legitimate and not uncommon. "The Battle Hymn of the Republic" rejoices in the hope of God taking vengeance. "Where is the Love" by Black Eyed Peas examines the hatred that often surrounds us today and cries out bitterly.

BIBLE**TRUTH** 3

Music can tell of love we have for another person. SONG OF SONGS 4:1-3

■ **Of the most popular songs today, how many would you say are love songs? List a few of them.**

INSIDE STORY: Song of Songs celebrates the love between a husband and wife. Solomon describes his love's beauty with agricultural metaphors (vv. 1, 2). The woman responds with another song, giving an equally romantic description of the king (5:10-13). It is clear that God created romantic love, and it is something to sing about. Adam responded with a love song when God created Eve (Genesis 2:23). A writer of Proverbs expressed his admiration and devotion to his wife (31:29, 30). Jesus made it clear that God is the author of marriage and even performed his first miracle at a wedding feast (Matthew 19:4-6; John 2:1-11). The writer of Hebrews clearly stated that God wanted marriage to be an honored and protected institution (Hebrews 13:4). God insists that romantic love be kept within his moral bounds. That would surely apply to songs about romantic love as well.

CHALLENGE

Encourage students to list some of their favorite songs and evaluate them biblically.

SCRIPTURE INDEX

OLD TESTAMENT

Genesis	Genesis 1:1	36
	Genesis 1:26, 27	82
	Genesis 1:28	36
	Genesis 1:31	82
	Genesis 2:15	36
	Genesis 2:18	14
	Genesis 2:23	86
	Genesis 3	22
	Genesis 3:1	62
	Genesis 3:17	82
	Genesis 3:21	36
	Genesis 9:20, 21	54
	Genesis 15:1-5	10
	Genesis 16:1-6	56
	Genesis 19:1, 12, 13	12
	Genesis 19:30-33	54
	Genesis 22:2	34
	Genesis 24:14-19	20
Exodus	Exodus 2:1-10	64
	Exodus 15:20, 21	48
	Exodus 20-23	26
	Exodus 22:21-27	42
	Exodus 23:12	51, 52
	Exodus 24:15-18	26
	Exodus 28:1	48
	Exodus 32:1-35	25, 26
	Exodus 34:9	66
Leviticus	Leviticus 19:14, 33, 34	42
	Leviticus 19:32-34	63, 64
Numbers	Numbers 12:1-15	47, 48
	Numbers 15:37-41	46
Deuteronomy	Deuteronomy 6:6-8	46
	Deuteronomy 6:13, 16	10
	Deuteronomy 8:3	10
	Deuteronomy 10:16	66
	Deuteronomy 19:15	76
	Deuteronomy 31:27	66
	Deuteronomy 32:4	40
	Deuteronomy 32:43	12
Joshua	Joshua 1:1-7	65, 66
	Joshua 2:1	66
	Joshua 2:2-4	20
	Joshua 12	66

Judges	Judges 2:12, 13	26
Ruth	Ruth 1:16-18	20
1 Samuel	1 Samuel 7:3	10
	1 Samuel 14:15	26
	1 Samuel 14:27, 29, 30	52
	1 Samuel 16:13	58
	1 Samuel 18:10-12	58
	1 Samuel 22:5	58
	1 Samuel 27:5-12	58
	1 Samuel 30:1-19	57, 58
	1 Samuel 30:11, 12	52
2 Kings	2 Kings 5:1-14	64
	2 Kings 8:25-27	68
	2 Kings 9:14-29	68
	2 Kings 11:1–12:2	67. 68
	2 Kings 18:23	10
	2 Kings 19:6, 7	10
2 Chronicles	2 Chronicles 20:2, 14, 15	10
Esther	Esther 2:7	68
Job	Job 24:1-4	86
	Job 31:1	43, 44
Psalms	Psalm 1:1-3	85, 86
	Psalm 8:1, 2	86
	Psalm 8:4-8	81, 82
	Psalm 9:1, 2	86
	Psalm 9:9	42
	Psalm 10:4	22
	Psalm 10:17, 18	42
	Psalm 12:5	41, 42
	Psalm 19:1	62
	Psalm 19:7-11	82
	Psalm 23:2, 3	52
	Psalm 24:3-5	72
	Psalm 34:8	10
	Psalm 73:2-26	55, 56
	Psalm 73:21-26	27, 28

	Psalm 84:10	60
	Psalm 90:2-10	82
	Psalm 90:9-12	60, 84
	Psalm 109:6-15	86
	Psalm 112:5	23, 24
	Psalm 118:1, 24	86
	Psalm 119:9, 11	62
	Psalm 119:103, 104	10
	Psalm 137:7-9	85, 86
	Psalm 139:13-16	41, 42
	Psalm 146:6	62
	Psalm 148:2-5	11, 12
	Psalm 149:4	22
Proverbs	Proverbs 1:1-7	61, 62
	Proverbs 1:10	26
	Proverbs 1:10-19	83, 84
	Proverbs 3:34	22
	Proverbs 8:13	22
	Proverbs 10:19	72
	Proverbs 11:2	22
	Proverbs 12:15	72
	Proverbs 12:16	76
	Proverbs 12:24	52
	Proverbs 13:10	22
	Proverbs 13:20	26
	Proverbs 16:18, 19	21, 22
	Proverbs 18:9	51, 52
	Proverbs 18:13	72
	Proverbs 19:15	52
	Proverbs 20:1	53, 54
	Proverbs 22:5	26
	Proverbs 23:20, 21	52
	Proverbs 24:1, 2	26
	Proverbs 24:13, 14	10
	Proverbs 29:25	25, 26
	Proverbs 31:4, 5	53, 54
	Proverbs 31:29, 30	86
Ecclesiastes	Ecclesiastes 9:10	60
	Ecclesiastes 10:16, 17	51, 52
	Ecclesiastes 11:9	59, 60
	Ecclesiastes 12:1	59, 60
Song of Songs	Song of Songs 4:1-3	85, 86
	Song of Songs 5:10-13	86
Isaiah	Isaiah 55:8	82
Jeremiah	Jeremiah 1:4, 5	41, 42
	Jeremiah 1:7	68
	Jeremiah 23:23	80
Daniel	Daniel 4:13	11, 12
Hosea	Hosea 6:6	80
Amos	Amos 5:15	86
Obadiah	Obadiah 6-9	86
Jonah	Jonah 4:1-11	56
Micah	Micah 6:6-8	80
Nahum	Nahum 3:1-4	86
Malachi	Malachi 3:10	24

NEW TESTAMENT

Matthew	Matthew 1:18-20	10
	Matthew 1:18-24	12
	Matthew 4:1-11	16, 72
	Matthew 4:11	12
	Matthew 5:13-16	63, 64
	Matthew 5:16	20
	Matthew 5:23-25	74
	Matthew 5:39-41	80
	Matthew 6:2-16	80
	Matthew 6:12	20
	Matthew 6:33	72
	Matthew 10:26, 27	83, 84
	Matthew 12:1, 2, 7, 8	79, 80
	Matthew 15:14	8
	Matthew 15:19	44
	Matthew 16:18	56
	Matthew 18:15-20	75, 76
	Matthew 19:4-6	86
	Matthew 21:12, 13	74
	Matthew 23	74
	Matthew 23:2-38	45, 46
	Matthew 28:18-20	66
	Matthew 28:19	48
Mark	Mark 5:15	50
	Mark 6:30, 31	52
	Mark 9:14-17, 28, 29	14
	Mark 10:45	24
	Mark 14:29-31	22
Luke	Luke 1:26-38	12
	Luke 2:19, 51	62
	Luke 4:1-13	9, 10
	Luke 7:36-50	28
	Luke 9:24-26	80
	Luke 12:1-7	78
	Luke 12:8-9	77, 78
	Luke 14:11	22
	Luke 15:10	12
	Luke 22:39-44	12
John	John 2:1-11	86
	John 4:21	79, 80
	John 4:24	80, 82
	John 6:1-15	64

	John 8:44	74
	John 9:4	59, 60
	John 10:7-11	77, 78
	John 12:23-26	80
	John 14:3	28
	John 14:6	74
	John 17:2, 23	8
Acts	Acts 2:42	16
	Acts 3:6, 7	78
	Acts 4:4-12	77, 78
	Acts 5:17, 18	8
	Acts 5:27-29	10
	Acts 8:26	12
	Acts 9:1, 2	8
	Acts 9:2-22	32
	Acts 9:26-28	31, 32
	Acts 10:34, 35	48
	Acts 11:19-21	30
	Acts 11:22-26	32
	Acts 12:1, 2	8
	Acts 12:6-10	12
	Acts 13:1	30
	Acts 13:1-3	32
	Acts 13:4-12	7, 8
	Acts 15:5	8
	Acts 16:1	68
	Acts 17:6, 7	70
	Acts 17:24	80
	Acts 17:24, 25	81, 82
	Acts 18:1-17	18
	Acts 19:13-16	13, 14
	Acts 20:17-31	23, 24
	Acts 24:16	70
	Acts 27:33, 34	52
	Acts 28:16-20	16
Romans	Romans 1:20	62, 82
	Romans 1:21	62
	Romans 1:22, 23	82
	Romans 2:4	62
	Romans 3:23	56, 74
	Romans 8:20-22	81, 82
	Romans 8:32, 33, 36, 37	80
	Romans 8:35-39	16
	Romans 9:1	62
	Romans 12:2	25, 26, 62
	Romans 12:3	50
	Romans 12:4-21	20
	Romans 13:1	22
	Romans 13:3-7	69, 70
	Romans 13:8	35, 36

	Romans 13:12-14	53, 54
	Romans 15:2	36
	Romans 15:5-7	31, 32
1 Corinthians	1 Corinthians 1:10	8
	1 Corinthians 2:1-10	17, 18
	1 Corinthians 5:10-13	76
	1 Corinthians 6:9-11	39, 40
	1 Corinthians 6:18	26
	1 Corinthians 7:21-24	30
	1 Corinthians 9:27	52
	1 Corinthians 10:13	54
	1 Corinthians 10:24	35, 36
	1 Corinthians 11:1	50
	1 Corinthians 15:33	84
2 Corinthians	2 Corinthians 2:14	50
	2 Corinthians 3:1-3	46
	2 Corinthians 4:4	7, 8
	2 Corinthians 5:5	34
	2 Corinthians 5:17	46
	2 Corinthians 6:2	60
	2 Corinthians 11:3	7, 8
	2 Corinthians 13:11	8
Galatians	Galatians 1:6, 7	8, 14
	Galatians 1:8	12
	Galatians 1:11-18	32
	Galatians 5:23	38
	Galatians 6:1	76
	Galatians 6:7	56, 84
Ephesians	Ephesians 2:14	30
	Ephesians 4:3-6	8
	Ephesians 4:15	40
	Ephesians 4:25-28	73, 74
	Ephesians 4:30	34
	Ephesians 5:1, 2, 25	34
	Ephesians 5:1-3	38
	Ephesians 5:4	53, 54
	Ephesians 5:15, 16	83, 84
	Ephesians 5:16	60
	Ephesians 5:21	22
	Ephesians 6:5-9	30
	Ephesians 6:10-18	15, 16
Philippians	Philippians 1:12-21	56
	Philippians 2:2	8
	Philippians 2:2, 3	24
	Philippians 2:3, 5	36
	Philippians 2:4	23, 24, 36
	Philippians 2:5-7	46
	Philippians 2:5-11	24
	Philippians 2:15	64
	Philippians 3:19	60

Colossians Colossians 2:13-16..................................14
Colossians 3:11......................................48
Colossians 3:16......................................86
Colossians 3:22-24................................30

1 Thessalonians 1 Thessalonians 1:5.............................62
1 Thessalonians 1:7.............................50
1 Thessalonians 4:1-8.....................37, 38
1 Thessalonians 4:11, 12..................63, 64

2 Thessalonians 2 Thessalonians 3:9.............................50
2 Thessalonians 3:11...........................64
2 Thessalonians 3:14...........................76

1 Timothy 1 Timothy 1:2..68
1 Timothy 4:1-5................................13, 14
1 Timothy 4:8..52
1 Timothy 4:12......................................68
1 Timothy 5:17......................................46
1 Timothy 5:23......................................54
1 Timothy 6:17......................................60

2 Timothy 2 Timothy 1:5..68
2 Timothy 1:7..66
2 Timothy 3:14, 15...............................66

Titus Titus 1:12..20, 44
Titus 1:12-14...52
Titus 2:4-6..44
Titus 2:6-8......................................49, 50
Titus 2:6-10..20
Titus 2:7...46
Titus 2:11, 12...................................43, 44

Philemon Philemon 8-16.................................29, 30

Hebrews Hebrews 1:14...................................11, 12
Hebrews 3:13..60
Hebrews 4:12..16
Hebrews 8:5..50
Hebrews 10:23-25.................................86
Hebrews 10:24..................................29, 30
Hebrews 12:22......................................12
Hebrews 13:2..12
Hebrews 13:4..86
Hebrews 13:7..46

James James 1:17...60
James 1:19-21...................................71, 72
James 1:26.......................................53, 54
James 2:19.......................................13, 14
James 3:5-6...72
James 3:17.......................................43, 44
James 4:1-20...72

1 Peter 1 Peter 2:17.....................................63, 64
1 Peter 2:15...............................16, 50, 70
1 Peter 2:18-21......................................30
1 Peter 2:21-23................................79, 80
1 Peter 3:1-8....................................19, 20
1 Peter 3:3, 4....................................43, 44
1 Peter 3:7.......................................35, 36
1 Peter 3:13..70
1 Peter 3:15.....................................16, 84
1 Peter 3:16..50
1 Peter 4:7..50
1 Peter 4:12..68
1 Peter 5:3......................................46, 50
1 Peter 5:5, 6...................................21, 22
1 Peter 5:8..68

2 Peter 2 Peter 2:1-3..8
2 Peter 2:14..60

1 John 1 John 2:1...78
1 John 2:9-11..20
1 John 2:11...8
1 John 3:19-22......................................50
1 John 4:4...66
1 John 4:7-21...................................33, 34

Jude Jude 3..16
Jude 6..14

Revelation Revelation 7:9...................................47, 48
Revelation 18..12
Revelation 19:11-16..............................16
Revelation 21:1.....................................82
Revelation 21:1-4..................................34
Revelation 22:15...................................40

SCRIPTURE TOPIC INDEX

A

Abortion 42
Accountability 30
Addiction 54
Adornment 20
Aggression 72
Alcohol 54
Angels 12, 14
Anger 72, 74, 86
Appetites 10
Armor of God 16
Arrogance 22, 46
Authority 70

B

Beauty 20, 44
Benevolence 64

C

Career 66
Character 20, 50
Cliques 32
Community 64
Confidence 18, 28
Conflict 76
Cursing 54

D

Deception 8, 10, 14
Demons 14
Depression 28, 56
Design 40
Devil 8, 10, 14, 16
Diet 52
Difficulty 68
Drugs 54
Dysfunction 68

E

Emotions 56
Evil 8, 10, 14, 16
Exclusion 32, 48
Exclusivity 78
Exercise 52

F

Failure 58
Family 68
Fear 10, 26
Fellowship 30
Forgiveness 40, 76
Friendship 30, 32

G

Generosity 24
Government 70

H

Habits 54
Health 52
Homosexuality 40
Humility 22
Hypocrisy 46

I

Idols 26
Inclusion 30, 32, 48
Integrity 50
Internet 84
Islam 80

K

Knowledge 62

L

Learning 62
Loneliness 28, 56
Love 34, 86
Love songs 86
Loyalty 30

M

Messenger 12
Mission 66
Morality 38, 40, 54
Music 86
Muslims 80

N

Nature 82

O

Obedience 70
One way 78
Online 84

P

Paganism 82
Peer pressure 26
Perseverance 58
Power 10, 22
Praise 86
Prejudice 48
Pride 22
Priorities 60
Problems 68
Profanity 54
Protection 12, 16
Purity 38, 44, 54
Purpose 66

R

Racism 48
Reconciliation 76
Relationships 30, 32, 34, 44, 76
Reputation 50
Respect 36
Rest 52, 60
Right to life 42

S

Salvation 78
Satan 8, 10, 14, 16
School 62
Self-control 44, 72
Self-esteem 18, 20, 28
Self-worth 18, 20, 28, 56
Sensuality 38, 40, 54
Service 24
Sexuality 38, 40, 54
Sincerity 50
Spirits 12, 14
Spiritual warfare 8, 10, 14, 16
Study 62
Submission 22, 34
Substance abuse 54
Surrender 34

T

Technology 84
Temper 72
Temptation 10, 26
Time 60, 84
Truth 78

U

Unborn 42
Unity 30, 32
Using others 36, 38

W

Wicca 82
Wisdom 62
Witchcraft 82
Work 64
Worship 12, 60

STORY TOPIC INDEX

A

Accident 35
Accomplishment 17
Adaptation...................................... 39
Addiction 53
Alcohol 49
Amazing Grace 33
Anger.................................. 55, 71, 75
Appetite 23
Applebee's 49
Arrogance 21
Atkinson, Gemma............................ 19

B

Back to School 61
Bald Eagle...................................... 23
Baseball 31
Beauty contest................................ 19
Benedict XVI.................................... 69
Blair, Tony 57
Bush, George W. 71

C

Cam'ron 25
Career 65
China 73
Chronicles of Narnia, The 67
Clean coal....................................... 37
Clean water 37
Coffee 53
Conflict... 75
Contest 7, 59
Cosmetics....................................... 19
Couch potato................................... 59
Creativity.. 39
Credit recovery 77
Crowned 19

D

Depression...................................... 27
Disability... 39
Disaster 63
Disaster relief 15
Dissent 73
Driving.. 21
Droopy pants................................... 47
Dysfunction..................................... 67

E

Earthquake 81
Emotions... 55
Engineers Without Borders 37
England.. 9, 57
ESPN Zone...................................... 59
Evil 13

F

Failure.. 57
First Amendment.............................. 73
Fisher, Carrie 69
Football 59
Fox hunting 9
Freedom of speech.......................... 73
Freedom of the press....................... 73
Funerals.. 35

G

Gas chambers 43
Genocide 43
Google.. 13
Great Britain 9, 57
Greed.. 23
Guns 83

H

Hanks, Tom 83
Harrison, George 39
Health 51
Healy, Jeff 39
Heroes 63
Hilton, Paris 19
Hogs 41
Hollywood 19

I

I-35W bridge collapse 63
Ig Nobel Prize 79
Immunizations 51
Imposter 45
Informant 25, 29
Insider trading 29
International law 69
Internet 13

J

Jagger, Mick 19
Johns Hopkins 53
Jolie, Angelina 19
Jones, Chipper 31

K

Kashmir Valley 31
Keith, Toby 69
King, B. B. 39
Knightley, Keira 19

L

Last respects 35
Law 47
Lewis, C.S. 67
Lil' Kim 25
Lite-Brite 17
Loopholes 69

M

Matthers, Jerry 69
Microchip 11
Military 15
Mission statement 13
Mix up 49
Moment of truth 9
Moon 69
Moss, Kate 19
Music 41, 85

N

Natchez, Mississippi 37
Natural disaster 35, 81
Nelson, Willie 69
Newton, John 33
Nixon, Richard 65
Nobel Prize 79

O

Outer space 7, 69

P

Pakistan 81
Paltrow, Gwyneth 19
Paterson, Governor David 71
Peer pressure 25
Pigs 41
Politics 57
Presley, Elvis 65
Prince Caspian 67

R

Real estate 69
Red Cross 15
Rescue 63
RFID 11
Rhymes, Busta 25
Road House 39

S

Safety 51
Saggy pants 47
Saturday Night Live 71
School 61, 77
Seat belts 51
Slavery 33
Sports 27
"Stand by Your Ham" 41
Stanford University 45
Starbucks 53
Star Trek 69
Stewart, Martha 29
Stop Snitchin' 25
Strategy 7
Stupid criminals 55
Swayze, Patrick 39

T

Temper..71, 75

Tornado..35

Tradition...9

Tragedy 35, 63

Transgressive art....................................43

Turning point 9

TV viewing 59

U

U.S. Constitution 73

W

Wilberforce, William................................33

Wildfires 15

Wildlife 23

World Baseball Classic............................31

World War II 43

Wynette, Tammy......................................41

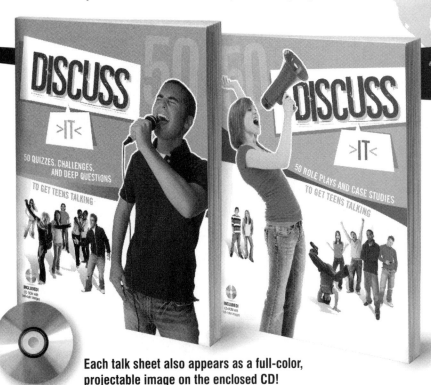